Sunset

HOUSEPLANTS

BY ROSEMARY McCREARY
AND THE EDITORS OF SUNSET BOOKS

SUNSET BOOKS • MENLO PARK, CALIFORNIA

DYNAMIC INDOOR GARDENS

Houseplants have journeyed far beyond the Victorian parlor palms of the 19th century and hanging ferns of the mid-20th. Today's nurseries and garden centers feature previously hard-to-find specimens for the novice and the seasoned indoor gardener alike—plants in flower at any time of year, dramatic *objet d'art* foliage plants, and hybrid cultivars destined to become collector's items for the ruffles of their petals or variegation on their leaves.

This book will help you select a houseplant and give you the cultural information and basic practices you'll want to follow in caring for it. We give you solutions to problems that may crop up, propagation tips, and formulas for mixing your own potting soil.

Once you've stepped into the living world of houseplants, try experimenting with a few exciting and unusual species—but don't despair if your early attempts aren't wildly successful. Instead, focus on the delight each plant gives you; dabble until you find foliage features, textures, and fragrances that you really like. And if some of your plants reveal shortcomings or disappoint you with their performance, simply replace them with more satisfying species.

We are grateful to many plant experts and nurseries for sharing their wealth of knowledge: Belisle's Violet House, Glasshouse Works, Grigsby Cactus Gardens, K & L Nursery, Kartuz Greenhouses, Sherry Olson, Rainbow Gardens, Rozell Rose Nursery & Violet Boutique, Vicki's Exotic Plants, and Volkmann Bros. Greenhouses. We especially want to thank Larry Hodgson of HortiCom Inc. for his expertise and valuable suggestions while reviewing the manuscript, and John R. Dunmire for contributing the pronunciation keys.

SUNSET BOOKS

Vice President, Sales: Richard A. Smeby
Editorial Director: Bob Doyle
Production Director: Lory Day
Art Director: Vasken Guiragossian

Staff for this book:

Managing Editor: Susan Bryant Caron
Sunset Books Senior Editor, Gardening: Suzanne Normand Eyre
Copy Editor and Indexer: Pamela A. Evans
Photo Researcher: Tishana Peebles
Production Coordinator: Patricia S. Williams
Special Contributors: Lisa Anderson, Jean Warboy
Proofreader: Jan deProsse, Eagle Eye Editorial Services

Art Director: Alice Rogers
Illustrator: Erin O'Toole
Computer Production: Fog Press, Linda Bouchard

Cover: A long-blooming African violet *(Saintpaulia)* and bright foliage *(Dracaena fragrans)* enliven indoor gardens.
Photography by Connie Toops.

PHOTOGRAPHERS

William D. Adams: 12 bottom right, 15 top right, 80 top right, 86 left, 98 left; **Greg Allikas:** 87 top right, bottom right; **Scott Atkinson:** 29, 36 right, 44 top right, back cover right; **R. S. Byther:** 47 left, 49 bottom; **Glenn Christiansen:** 65 left; **Richard Clark:** 89 middle right; **Crandall & Crandall:** 8 top left, 10 top left, 23 top right, 45 bottom, 46 bottom left, 47 bottom right, top center, bottom center, 49 third from top, 58 right, 60 top left, 62 left, 67 top right, 78 middle left, bottom left, 83 left, 94 middle left, 107 bottom right; **Jim Cummings:** 10 bottom left, 12 bottom left, 91 top; **Arnaud Descat/M.A.P.:** 1, 6 top left, 7 center left, 14 top left, top right, 16 center left, 17 top right, 54 top, 59 bottom, 63 left, 64 top left, 67 bottom right, 68 right, 72 left, bottom right, 75 bottom right, 78 top left, right, 79 bottom left, middle right, 82 right, 86 right, 88 right, 89 top right, 90 middle left, top right, 99 top right, middle right, 100 bottom, 103 left, 108 bottom left; **Alan and Linda Detrick:** 6 top center, top right, bottom center, 7 bottom right, 8 bottom left, bottom right, 9 bottom left, top right, center right, bottom right, 11 top left, middle left, 14 bottom left, 20 top left, 22, 23 top left, 27, 33 bottom, 39 bottom left, 40 left, 47 top right, 54 bottom, 74 bottom left, 79 top right, 81 right, 89 bottom left, 90 top left, bottom right, 92 bottom left, 95 bottom, 97 bottom, 99 bottom right, 101 bottom right, 102 top, 103 bottom right, 104 bottom left, 107 middle right, 108 right; **Frédéric Didillon/M.A.P.:** 13 top right, 15 top left, 102 bottom; **Derek Fell:** 2, 3 bottom right, 6 middle right, 7 top center, center, top right, center right, 11 top center, 12 top right, 14 center right, 20 bottom left, 25 bottom left, 46 bottom center, bottom right, 52, 55 top, 56 bottom, 57 bottom left, 60 middle left, bottom left, 63 middle right, 69, 70 right, 71 top right, 72 top right, 77, 79 bottom right, 84 right, 85 right, 87 left, 89 left, 92 right, 94 right, 96 top left, bottom, 97 top, middle, 100 top, 101 top left, top right, 104 top left, middle left, 105 top right, bottom center, 106 bottom, bottom right, 107 middle right, 109 top, 110 top right, bottom left, bottom right, back cover top left; **Paul Hammond:** 92 top left; **Larry Hodgson, HortiCom Inc.:** 7 bottom center, 14 third from top right, 24 left, 28, 57 top right, 59 top, 60 top right, 61 top center, left, 65 top right, 66 bottom left, 71 bottom right, 74 top left, 75 left, top right, 80 bottom right, 83 right, 85 left, 105 left, 106 top left; **Saxon Holt:** 3 top right, bottom left, 14 bottom center, 16 top, 17 center, bottom right, 18, 23 bottom left, 25 left, 34, 39 top, 45 top, center, 84 left; **Horticultural Photography:** 11 bottom center, 99 left; **Hydrofarm Gardening Products, Petaluma, CA:** 24 right; **Bill Johnson:** 49 second from top, 50 bottom, 61 center left, center right, 64 third from top left, bottom left, 65 bottom right, 66 top left, 81 left, 104 right, 105 second from top right, 106 top right; **P. Johnson:** 63 bottom right; **Fred Lamarque/M.A.P.:** 110 top left; **J. Lodé/M.A.P.:** 62 right; **Steve W. Marley:** 61 bottom, 64 right, 103 top right; **Ells W. Marugg:** 56 top, 63 top right, 76 bottom, 94 bottom left, 103 middle right, 105 bottom right, 108 top left; **N. and P. Mioulane/M.A.P.:** 3 top left, 4, 14, 17 bottom left, 21, 26 right, 33 top, 38, 44 left, bottom right, 46 top center, second from top center, 50 top, 64 second from top left, 66 right, 71 left, 93 top; **Yann Monel/M.A.P.:** 20 top right, 42; **Orchids of Los Osos:** 11 right; **Norman A. Plate:** 9 top left, 13 bottom right, center right, 15 bottom left, 16 bottom left, 30, 31, 32, 36 left, 39 bottom right, 40 top right, bottom right, 41, 43, 57 bottom right, 58 top left, 68 left, 80 top left, bottom left, 90 bottom left; **Mae Scanlan:** 17 top left, 25 top left; **Joseph G. Strauch, Jr.:** 14 far bottom right, 58 bottom left, 73, 82 left, 88 left, 93 bottom, 94 top left, 96 top right, 98 right, 106 middle left, 107 top right, 109 bottom; **David Stubbs:** 91 bottom; **Michael S. Thompson:** 70 left; **Connie Toops:** 49 top, 55 bottom, 76 top, 79 top left, 95 top, 105 third from top right; **Tom Woodward:** 15 bottom right; **Tom Wyatt:** 8 center right, 10 right, 60 bottom right, back cover bottom left.

CONTENTS

INDOOR
GARDENS

Houseplants lend an ambience and distinction to our homes and workplaces that no other decorative element can deliver. Though artificial plant substitutes abound, the luster and freshness of living plants remains unmatched. Besides bestowing their grace on our tabletops, corners, and bay windows, houseplants can satisfy that instinct to garden even if available space is limited to a sunny windowsill. Really avid indoor gardeners will push beyond such apparent limitations, however—rearranging furniture to catch or block seasonal changes in sunlight, seeking out resilient plants for difficult interiors, and taking delight in the rare and unusual.

You can use houseplants boldly—choosing ficus, palms, and giant century plants to enliven entire rooms— or you can adopt a simpler style—a medicinal aloe, a cactus dish garden, or a practical pot of parsley. Whichever plants you favor, take the time to learn their basic requirements, for their origins are as diverse as frigid, high plateaus and steamy, tropical rain forests. In truth, their very existence is completely dependent on how you manipulate their artificial indoor environment. With the right care, your plants will respond readily as they enchant and reward you with stately, graceful foliage and abundant blooms.

Hibiscus, hydrangea, bougainvillea, and fuchsia intermingle
with an array of dramatic foliage plants, transforming a sunroom into an indoor garden.

BEYOND GREEN

The reliably green foliage of houseplants refreshes a tired decor or sets off a lively one as nothing else can. Many plants, though, are not merely green. Some resonate with vibrant foliage tones and multi-hued variegation, abandoning green altogether. Others bloom in bashful pastels or create splashy accents with their colorful blossoms, replacing cut flowers as indoor bouquets.

If you are looking for something beyond the ordinary, you may want to journey forth on a new plant–hunting venture: try a few fanciful and floriferous species such as cape primrose *(Streptocarpus)* and columnea, and then move on to the host of orchid options. But when time is a constraint, you needn't look further than your local garden center or supermarket to find traditional blooming favorites like geraniums *(Pelargonium)*, gloxinia *(Sinningia)*, and Christmas cactus *(Schlumbergera)*. These will regularly pop into bloom to supply long periods of charming color.

Bright caladium foliage

If steady, dependable color is what you seek, turn to the dynamic world of foliage plants. Exciting shades of green abound—forest, emerald, olive, chartreuse, aquamarine—but the truly remarkable plants are more than green. Some light up a room quietly with serenely pale leaves and softly hued, exquisite variegation; others blaze out in glory, a few in shockingly assertive tones. Choose from a wide spectrum of iridescent purple, cream and burgundy, silver stripes and speckles, vibrant red, rose, and more to transform your indoor garden into an exotic scene year-round. As you add to your collection, "in living color" will take on new meaning—one that becomes an extension of your own personality and green thumb.

CLOCKWISE, FROM TOP LEFT: Sprightly cape primrose *(Streptocarpus)* and African violets *(Saintpaulia)* bloom nearly constantly indoors. Amaryllis *(Hippeastrum)* and poinsettia *(Euphorbia pulcherrima)* brighten an indoor winter landscape, framed by a variegated ivy *(Hedera)* and a large-leafed philodendron. Croton *(Codiaeum)* foliage glistens with a range of hues every month of the year.

PLANTS FOR INDOOR BLOOM

Aechmea	*Orchids*
Begonia	*Pelargonium*
Clerodendrum	*Saintpaulia*
Clivia	*Schlumbergera*
Cyclamen	*Sinningia*
Guzmania	*Spathiphyllum*
Hippeastrum	*Streptocarpus*

LEFT: Dazzling foliage plants rival the showy blossoms of a winter-flowering begonia.

LEFT, BELOW: Dieffenbachia, dracaena, peperomia, and other foliage plants light up a room year-round with bright color, rich texture, and varied pattern.

RIGHT, BELOW: *Peperomia caperata* 'Variegated Ripple' and *Fittonia verschaffeltii*

PLANTS WITH COLORFUL FOLIAGE

Begonia	*Maranta*
Caladium	*Neoregelia*
Codiaeum	*Peperomia*
Dieffenbachia	*Solenostemon*
Dracaena	*Tradescantia*
Fittonia	*Vriesea*
Gynura	
Hypoestes	
Iresine	

ABOVE: Foliage alone fills this sunroom with bright color.

RIGHT, TOP TO BOTTOM: Coleus (*Solenostemon scutellarioides* 'Texas Parking Lot') and the rex begonia 'Silver Queen' produce masses of vivid color tones.

EASY-CARE COMPANIONS

Indoor gardening couldn't be easier than it is with durable, low-light foliage plants—unless, that is, you are growing an equally carefree begonia or pelargonium. Plants featured in the lists on these pages are a few of the nonfussy stars that have long reigned supreme in homes and offices because of their amiable nature. Easy-care houseplants range from bold, leather-leafed, tree-size figs (Ficus), dracaenas, and giant philodendrons to airy, cascading spider plants (Chlorophytum); from hundreds of species of desert cacti to other curious succulents of every type. Don't let delicate looks or audacious size fool you—all of these plants are undemanding in character and effortless to live with. Forgiveness may be their greatest virtue; they allow you to make mistakes without incurring fatalities!

EASY-CARE PLANTS

Aspidistra	*Pelargonium*
Begonia	*Philodendron*
Bromeliads	*Sansevieria*
Cacti	*Spathiphyllum*
Chlorophytum	Succulents
Cissus	*Syngonium*
Dieffenbachia	*Tradescantia*
Dracaena	
Epipremnum	

Lustrous foliage and exotic tropical flowers aren't always easy to maintain, but these plants make few demands.

CLOCKWISE, FROM TOP LEFT: Trailing grape ivy (*Cissus*), the torchlike blooms of bromeliad *Guzmania* 'Grapeade', a long-blooming succulent kalanchoe, and peace lily (*Spathiphyllum*)

LOW-LIGHT PLANTS

Aglaonema	*Ficus*
Araucaria	*Fittonia*
Aspidistra	*Monstera*
Caladium	*Palms*
Cissus	*Philodendron*
Dracaena	*Sansevieria*
Ferns	*Syngonium*

Keep in mind that tough survivors don't have to look the part to fit the role. You might guess that an armed, spiny cactus or succulent euphorbia can fend for itself over long periods, but who would suspect that a plant with so tender a name as queen's tears *(Billbergia nutans)* can do the same? Or that a leafy stem of epipremnum can live for years in a glass of water—in case you never get around to potting it up?

If you keep a busy schedule or have a room with low light, by all means seek out easy-care plants. Rest assured that there is a multitude of shade lovers just perfect for that dim corner in an otherwise bright room, or where windows are shadowed by an overhanging roof, or for windowless, artificially lit locations. Some houseplants, in fact, will simply not tolerate bright sunlight. Many more drought-tolerant species abhor too-frequent watering—those species are even easier to live with.

TOP AND BOTTOM LEFT: This jungle cactus (top) and these desert cacti (bottom) adapt readily to indoor conditions, flourishing with minimal care.

TOP RIGHT: The multihued Chinese evergreen (*Aglaonema commutatum* 'Maria') thrives in low-light situations.

MIDDLE RIGHT: *Dracaena deremensis* 'Lemon and Lime' withstands a range of conditions and is a winner valued for its easy nature.

BOTTOM RIGHT: It's hard to go wrong with a rubber plant *(Ficus elastica)*. Its lustrous foliage tolerates lower light and less water than most other plants do—and even a little neglect.

VERTICAL POSES AND GRACEFUL CASCADES

Enter the dramatic: pendent trails of leafy stems and blossom clusters; tall, twisted trunks with swordlike leaves; lofty sprays of palm and fern fronds. Plants with these vertical dimensions—whether dangling downward or ascending on tall stalks—are perfect in spacious and high-ceilinged rooms, where they fill interior space in a unique way, often providing striking architectural effects.

A few treelike houseplants are, in fact, trees, but most never grow out-of-bounds when confined indoors. The popular weeping fig *(Ficus benjamina)* usually stays small if its roots are confined; in large containers or planter beds in an enclosed atrium, it may grow 20 feet or more. You can achieve the same vertical drama that a tree confers by giving hoya or twining ivy *(Hedera)* a trellis or post to climb and training its dangling stems into an upright position.

You'll want to be sure you have ready access to all hanging plants, in order to carry out watering and maintenance chores. Plants on balcony ledges are easy to reach, but those suspended above normal ceiling height are not. Dragging a ladder around the house may seem like a workable notion at first, but you will soon tire of it. You may be able to purchase or contrive a pulley for raising and lowering such hanging containers with little effort. In any case, look for the least intrusive kinds of supports for your hanging plants; sturdy hangers come in nearly invisible thin metal strips and clear plastic filament.

ABOVE: Fishtail palm *(Caryota mitis)*

LEFT: Weeping fig *(Ficus benjamina* 'Wintergreen')

PLANTS FOR VERTICAL ACCENTS

Clerodendrum	*Hoya*
Coffea	*Monstera*
Cordyline	*Musa*
Dracaena	*Palms*
Epipremnum	*Philodendron*
Ferns	*Schefflera*
Ficus	

Paradise palm *(Howea forsteriana)*

LEFT, TOP TO BOTTOM: Spider plant *(Chlorophytum comosum* 'Vittatum') and English ivy *(Hedera helix)*

CENTER TOP: More graceful than its name implies, the burro's tail *(Sedum morganianum)* is a distinctive addition to any room.

CENTER BOTTOM: Arrowhead plant *(Syngonium podophyllum)*

RIGHT: This *Cuitlauzina pendula* orchid fills its arching and cascading stems with lemon-scented blossoms.

PLANTS THAT DRAPE OR TRAIL

Achimenes	*Orchids*
Aeschynanthus	*Plectranthus*
Callisia	*Saxifraga*
Chlorophytum	*Sedum*
Cissus	*Senecio*
Epipremnum	*Syngonium*
Hedera	*Tradescantia*
Hoya	

RIGHT: Choose plants from a rainbow of colors for holiday gift giving. Red and white poinsettias are always popular, but you'll also find (left to right) tuberous begonia, cyclamen, iris, tulips, yellow poinsettia, and sinningia.

BELOW: A gift of a Norfolk Island pine *(Araucaria heterophylla)* keeps on giving for decades.

GIFTS FROM THE FLORIST

A stunning potted plant from the florist makes a perfect gift for a gardener. Don't be disappointed, however, when you trim off faded blossoms or foliage and remove the glittery wrap to find your plant looking quite ordinary, even a little drab. You probably received it in its finest hour, fresh from the hothouse. After a bit of a rest, a summer growth period (out-of-doors is best), and a dose of fertilizer, your plant will regain its original beauty. The special needs of some common gift plants are noted in the listings that follow to help you revive them for subsequent seasons. Additional care instructions for orchids and other suitable gift plants are given in "Favorite Houseplants" (pages 53–110).

ACHIMENES. Cupid's bower, or magic flower, is related to African violets and gloxinia and hence requires similar care. A beautiful mass of foliage and flowers, this plant needs protection from sun and wind if moved out-of-doors. In autumn, remove the rhizome and let it dry out; store it in a cool, dry location and then repot it in spring.

Achimenes 'Jewel Pink'

ARAUCARIA HETEROPHYLLA. A distinctive, nonblooming conifer, slow-growing Norfolk Island pine bears its branches in graceful tiers and makes a lovely small-scale Christmas tree. Given good drainage, cool temperatures, and ample light, this unique plant can remain in the same pot indoors for years. You can grow it outside in very mild climates; elsewhere, confine its outdoor adventures to summer visits.

CALADIUM BICOLOR. Its vivid, paper-thin leaves make caladium a standout houseplant and a striking addition to other foliage plants needing little light, whether indoors or out. Capable of reaching 2 to 4 feet, this large-leafed wonder enjoys the same care as tuberous begonias: frequent misting and light applications of fertilizer. Store its dry tubers over winter and replant them in spring.

CYCLAMEN PERSICUM. Florist's cyclamen makes an elegant gift plant. Its bright flowers resembling shooting stars stand above the heart-shaped, attractively mottled foliage. Its extended bloom period lasts longest when it's given a cool location with bright light (no direct sun) and constantly moist soil. After the blossoms fade, let the foliage die back; moisten the soil lightly every few weeks. After it rests for a few months, replant the tuber (preferably in late summer) with the top just above the soil mix; resume watering and fertilizing. In mild climates, you can plant it out-of-doors.

GARDENIA AUGUSTA. Famous for its richly perfumed flowers and glossy, dark green leaves, gardenia needs regular fertilizing, bright light (but not intense sun), and more water than do most houseplants. Although gardenias benefit from spending hot summer days out-of-doors, their blooms will be most bountiful if you maintain an even temperature—62° to 65°F (17° to 19°C)—and humidity level while the buds are forming.

STRELITZIA REGINAE. Bird of paradise blooms intermittently all year, producing long-lasting, exotic flowers of orange, blue, and white atop long, stiff stems. Indoors or out, it does best in sun (but light shade in hot climates) and average to warm temperatures, with frequent heavy fertilizing and regular water. Set it outside for the summer, but never allow it to be exposed to frost.

NEXT YEAR'S BLOOMS

A few plants from the florist can go right into the garden in most climates, after you've enjoyed their flowers indoors: chrysanthemums and Easter lilies are two examples.

Cut off the faded blooms of the popular potted mums, leaving the stems 6 to 8 inches long. After moistening the soil thoroughly, separate the roots and set the plants outside in a sunny bed whenever the soil is workable. Though chrysanthemums bloom year-round at the florist's, your garden plants will flower in autumn.

When your Easter lily fades, snip off its blossoms but leave all of the foliage intact. Plant it outside in deep, porous soil where it will have ample moisture along with good drainage. Give the foliage full or filtered sun; mulch the roots to shade them. Once established, your lily will bloom each year—but in midsummer, not at Easter.

ONE-SEASON HOUSEPLANTS

Not all potted florist's plants are long-lived. A few are either annuals or plants that never recover from a seasonal display. Some can be coaxed to perform again, but require more effort than you may feel they're worth. Here are a few examples.

Ornamental pepper, *Capsicum annuum*, is really a summer-garden vegetable that, given bright light, makes a fabulous show as a houseplant and winter holiday decoration. Peppers obscure the small stems, blanketing them with yellow that turns to brilliant red. When all the fruit has dropped, the by-now-woody plants can be discarded.

Impatiens hybrids are extremely long-blooming annuals, given the right conditions: confined roots, bright but indirect light, moderate temperatures, and regular fertilizing. Most begin to look leggy and unsightly by late fall, when they should be discarded and replaced with young plants grown from tip cuttings taken in the summer. If you didn't take cuttings, purchase young nursery-grown plants again in the spring.

The popular poinsettia, *Euphorbia pulcherrima*, is theoretically a candidate for rebloom after a year out of the winter holiday spotlight. Some determined and disciplined gardeners are able to nurture it for months and then manipulate its exposure to light and darkness just enough to turn its showy bracts bright red again. But for most of us, it's best to purchase a pot fresh from commercial growers each year.

TOP: To send a touch of the tropics, give the long-lasting blooms of bird of paradise (here, *Strelitzia reginae* 'Banks').

ABOVE: A miniature cymbidium orchid (here, Golden Elf 'Sunburst') makes a beautiful and fragrant gift.

BELOW: Ornamental peppers *(Capsicum annuum)* spice up indoor decors with hot colors and flavorful fruits.

The bromeliad
Vriesea carinata

UNUSUAL PLANTS

Bromeliads
Cacti
Calathea
Carnivorous plants
Caudiciforms
Gynura
Mimosa
Orchids
Succulents

WEIRD AND WONDERFUL

Plants, like people, are often endearing not so much for their beauty as for their character. Such is the case with the sampling of botanical oddities listed at left, which have delighted imaginative gardeners for years. They're especially fun for children, who may learn from one of these intriguing plants to enjoy more conventional ones.

Eccentric, curious, strange, surprising, unconventional, even weird—no matter how you describe these plants, they're sure to be conversation pieces. Besides standing out by virtue of their arresting shapes and habits, they can "organize" a room by drawing the eye to their location and thus emphasizing that particular area. Display your specimen where it can pull your guests right into your horticultural world by prompting the question, "What's *that?*"

ABOVE: Looking for a plant with uncommon interest? These intriguing leaves and stems never go unnoticed: Venus fly trap, *Dionaea muscipula* (top); *Opuntia clavarioides* (middle); and *Tillandsia ionantha* (bottom).

RIGHT: *Pachypodium brevicaule*

LEFT: Spider orchid (*Brassia gireoudiana*)

Ponytail palm *(Nolina recurvata)*

OUTDOOR PLANTS INDOORS

In cold-winter climates, the subject of houseplants is much more compelling than it is where tender perennials and shrubs grow in the ground year-round. Cold weather sends even large vines and shrubs like bougainvillea and hibiscus scuttling inside, where they take on a new identity as parlor plants and put on showy, late-winter blooms. Not all indoor/outdoor plants are so obliging, but some do give spectacular performances. It's hard to beat the haze of pink covering a jade plant or the charm of a fuchsia flowering indoors in winter—especially when the view outside is bleak and chilling!

Tender outdoor plants such as pelargoniums (top), hibiscus (above), and fuchsia (right) need a transitional resting period to adjust to warmer indoor temperatures and lower light levels.

If you are lucky enough to have a glassed greenhouse, moving tender perennials and shrubs indoors is a fairly simple transition. Make-do arrangements, however, can work nearly as well. As long as you give your plants at least half a day of good light, friendly winter quarters can be arranged in an extra bedroom, a sunporch, or a bay window. If you lack such spaces, you may be able to set up grow lights in a basement or heated garage to overwinter some of your favorites. Remember that, though you didn't need to turn your pots when they sat outside in diffused light, you will need to rotate them periodically indoors.

Plants that spend half the year in and half out must be treated differently from most standard houseplants. Give them the same care that you would if they were planted permanently in the ground; that is, prune them back annually to remove dead wood and promote dense growth, watch for migrating pests and apply specific controls outside before you bring them in, and be prepared to protect them from unseasonably low or high temperatures. As you do houseplants, keep them well watered and fertilized during their growing seasons.

EASING THE MOVE

Plants that remain evergreen through winter shouldn't be moved abruptly into a warm area; give them a few days in a transitional zone, such as a protected porch. (Deciduous plants that go dormant in winter will be less sensitive.) Because the months spent indoors will be stressful for these plants, withhold fertilizer and monitor watering carefully through the winter. The soil should never be soggy, nor should it dry out completely. Once their growing season begins again in spring, resume fertilizing your plants before they go out-of-doors. When all danger of frost is past, move them outside gradually to harden them off and prevent damage to their tender new growth.

INDOOR/OUTDOOR PLANTS

Abutilon	Mandevilla
Agapanthus	Pelargonium
Azalea	Trachelospermum
Bougainvillea	
Fuchsia	
Hibiscus	
Hydrangea	
Impatiens	
Jade plant and other succulents	

Agapanthus 'Peter Pan'

AMAZING MINIATURES

With the introduction of the many new miniatures, indoor gardening in small spaces no longer need exclude roses. These little charmers can grow surprisingly tall—2 feet or more—so choose yours carefully if you want to put it in a greenhouse window or maintain it in a tiny pot on a window ledge. Miniatures are usually sold according to their size and habit; look for cultivars described as low or small. The microminis will stay under 1 foot.

Though these tiny hybrids really aren't meant to be houseplants, they may bring you months and even years of pleasure indoors. Their preferred culture is outside and in the ground, but with adequate moisture, exposure to sunlight, and good air circulation they can remain vigorous for some time. (For greatest longevity, move mature plants out-of-doors seasonally, bringing them indoors for winter only.) As indoor plants, they need a half-strength dose of liquid fertilizer every few weeks during active growth; also mist them frequently or hold them upside down under gently running water. Give your roses a 6- to 8-week colder rest period in the winter; at that time, be sure to keep the soil lightly moist and to withhold fertilizer.

TRULY TINY ROSES

You can find the smallest of the miniatures, the 6- to 8-inch-tall microminis, in supermarket nurseries, garden centers, gift shops, and mail-order catalogs. New cultivars appear each year; here are some winners.

'Baby Darling' (orange with a yellow reverse)

'Cinderella' (very double white; pink tints in cool weather)

'Elfinglo' (double magenta mauve; profuse and long lasting)

'Larado' (single, bright red; compact)

'Little Meghan' (bright yellow; an award winner)

'Lynne Gold' (deep yellow; tiny buds)

'Red Rosamini' (profuse red blooms; a good performer)

'Trinket' (rose pink; good for mini-arrangements)

Miniature roses vary from teacup size to small shrubs. Their flowers and foliage may likewise be small or large. A self-watering pot (bottom left) prevents the minis and microminis from drying out too quickly.

FORCING BULBS

Some of the most exciting indoor blossoms don't appear on traditional houseplants; rather, they are the extravagant results of manipulating, or "forcing," bulbs into bloom in winter or early spring. Although not all bulbs will respond well to forcing, many of the most popular spring bloomers do. When browsing through catalogs or shopping in your local nursery, look for species and varieties described as good for forcing. The largest, top-quality bulbs will give you the most satisfying results—they have the most stored energy and will yield the best blooms.

Some bulbs, because of their native origin, need to experience pronounced cold before they can produce a flowering stem. Check with your supplier to see how long yours were prechilled before you purchased them. Most cold-requiring bulbs need additional treatment after purchase. Chilling temperatures should be between 35° and 50°F (2° and 10°C) for the best foliage and flowers. Try an old refrigerator, unheated basement or garage, service porch, cold frame, or trench dug in the ground and lined with hardware cloth to keep burrowing critters away. For more detailed information on forcing bulbs, see the *Sunset* book *Bulbs.*

Bulbs forced once cannot be forced again. If you want to plant your bulbs in the ground after they've bloomed, first make sure they'll perform well in your climate. Keep the pots well watered, but set them aside until the foliage dies back. It may take a few seasons in the garden for them to recover from the stress of being forced, because they have lost nearly all of their stored energy; don't expect the same showstopping performance anytime soon. Many gardeners simply discard their forced bulbs in favor of fresh new ones each spring.

Force bulbs for indoor bloom in a shallow pot—ideally, one wider than deep, but at least twice as deep as the largest bulb. You may want to try a specialty container, such as a hyacinth glass or the crocus pot shown at right.

CLOCKWISE, FROM TOP LEFT: Amaryllis *(Hippeastrum)*, hyacinths, Dutch hybrid crocuses, mixed bulbs, and *Narcissus* 'Totus albus'.

BULBS TO CHILL

These bulbs need to be chilled for 3 months before they can be forced into early bloom.

Allium	*Hyacinthus*
Anemone blanda	*orientalis*
Camassia	*Ipheion uniflorum*
Chionodoxa	*Iris*
Convallaria majalis	*(reticulata types)*
Crocus	*Leucojum*
(early-blooming	*Muscari*
types)	*Narcissus*
Eranthis hyemalis	*Scilla* (except
Fritillaria meleagris	*S. peruviana*)
Galanthus	*Tulipa*

BULBS READY FOR FORCING

These bulbs are native to mild-winter areas, so they do not need chilling.

Anemone coronaria	*Iris* (Dutch hybrids)
Colchicum	*Narcissus*
Crocus	*(paper whites)*
(fall-blooming types)	*Ranunculus*
Freesia	*asiaticus*
Hippeastrum	*Scilla peruviana*

GETTING STARTED

Choosing the right plant for the right place means selecting one that can thrive in the conditions you have in your home. In its natural setting, a plant adapts to seasonal fluctuations of light levels, moisture and dryness, and temperature. Inside your home, however, those changes tend to be minimal. Houseplants undergo different kinds of adjustments and, consequently, a certain amount of stress. You can keep stress to a minimum by choosing appropriate plants and providing them with the best kind of nurturing: tender, loving care.

A sunny porch is ideal for isolating new plants before adding them to your houseplant collection. In winter, move plants there for a period of cool rest.

FIRST STEPS

It's safest to buy from a reputable nursery, garden center, or florist, where you can be sure that the plants have received continuous proper care. Remember, the best buys may not be the best bargains—if you have any doubts at all, don't buy. It pays to be choosy; healthy, mature plants will give you the most enjoyment with minimal effort in the least amount of time.

When you're ready to buy, look for a plant with dense, richly colored foliage and a well-formed root mass. There should be no evidence of pest or disease damage. Always avoid purchasing plants with leggy growth that gives the illusion of size but lacks strength. Wilted or yellowing leaves, too, may indicate damaged roots; brown spots or browned leaf edges could reflect either disease or underwatering.

Here are a few tips for purchasing a prospective houseplant.

A well-nurtured Boston fern (*Nephrolepis exaltata* 'Bostoniensis') and bromeliad (*Neoregelia carolinae* 'Tricolor')

 ∽ Survey the entire selection of a nursery or garden center. Do most of its plants seem healthy? An attractive overall look usually means that plants have received proper care from the beginning.

 ∽ Examine the plant itself, checking its leaves, stems, and—if possible—roots. Look for potential problems, as well as for new growth, good color, and a balanced shape. Avoid plants with broken parts and those whose roots protrude from the drainage holes.

 ∽ Choose a plant that's close to the size you want, rather than buying a small one and waiting for it to grow—that could take months or years.

 ∽ Purchase a compatible potting mix and fertilizer when you buy your plant. With these on hand, you'll be ready for maintenance chores.

EVALUATING A POTENTIAL PURCHASE

LEFT: Always start with a vigorous plant.

RIGHT: Diseased or weakened plants are never a bargain, even at a reduced price; they rarely recover their good health.

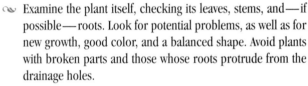

MAKING THE TRANSITION

Take a two-step approach to easing your plant into its new home in order to cushion the shock of moving it from the greenhouse. Your plant has been heavily fertilized to prepare it for the marketplace, leaving it with unknown quantities of residues that could burn its roots and leaves. Therefore, first flush the soil with one or two good waterings to remove accumulated salt residues. (Skip this step for low-water plants such as cacti.)

Second, give your plant a rest in isolation for a week or two while you observe it. Even though you checked for potential pest problems at purchase time, taking this precautionary step will protect your other plants from any lingering infestation.

PLANNING FOR CHANGES

Once your plant is well situated in its new home, look around for alternative growing sites. Many species grow best in one location during summer, but in a different one during winter. That's because winter is the usual resting time for most houseplants, when the days shorten and the sunlight is less intense. Some houseplants need cooler temperatures at this time; a few actually drop their leaves. Watch for signs of slowing activity late in the season; cut back then on watering and fertilizing while maintaining the same humidity level.

Keep in mind that plants' adaptation to seasonal changes is a natural and even necessary process. During dormancy, for example, they produce less food and slow their growth. Trying to force them, with fertilizer and light, to grow and flower during that resting period can actually be detrimental to them. You may want to set aside an area for plants "at rest," where you can give them special attention. Keep dormant tubers, bulbs, and corms there as well: these should dry out, but never completely (if kept too moist, they will rot). Note that cyclamen is an exception to the usual pattern, entering dormancy in summer; see page 12.

When interior light diminishes in winter, especially in northern climates, move plants that grow year-round into brighter light. A hobby greenhouse provides an ideal alternative environment.

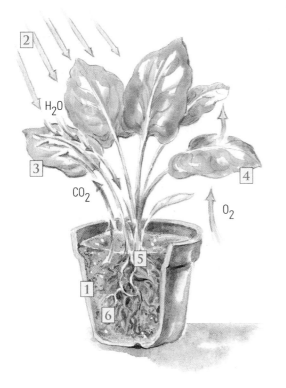

HOW PLANTS GROW

Although the needs and habits of individuals vary, all plants undergo the same growth processes.

1   The roots absorb water as moisture evaporates from the leaves into dry air.

2   Light provides energy for photosynthesis.

3   Carbon dioxide and water are used in photosynthesis to produce sugar.

4   Oxygen is taken in for respiration in all plant parts; it is given off as a by-product of photosynthesis in leaves and stems.

5   Loose soil holds both air and water.

6   Roots are healthiest and grow best when soil fills the pot; there should be no gravel in the bottom to take up root space.

LIGHT

SEASONAL CHANGES

As the angle of the sun's rays changes throughout the year, you may need to move your plants away from or closer to a window. South-facing windows see the greatest amount of seasonal change. Actually, more light enters your windows in winter, when the angle of the sun's rays is lowest, though its intensity is less than in summer. Nearly all plants can tolerate some southern exposure in winter, and those thriving on bright western and eastern light in summer especially may need to be moved to a southern exposure when the sun drops in the sky.

In wintertime it's safe to move plants from cooler northern exposures to east-facing windows, and to move those that normally thrive in higher heat in eastern exposures to southern or western rooms, which are warmer from the sun's radiant heat.

For proper growth, all plants need light—but the amount required varies from one species to another. Whereas outdoor plants are categorized as sun or shade lovers, houseplants are grouped according to their need for bright or low light. Only a few like direct sun; most do best in bright light that is indirect or filtered. If your conditions fall short of a plant's needs, consider supplementing the available natural light with artificial light devoted specifically to your plants.

Blooming and fruiting plants, as well as those with variegated leaves, require the brightest light indoors; plants with solid green foliage tend to prefer lower light. The intensity of the light is as important as the length of daily exposure to it. And the effect of these factors must be judged over the long term, because most plants can tolerate poor conditions for a few weeks. Any plant that shrivels or develops tan or brown spots may be getting too much direct light. Plants that lean to one side, grow only on one side, fail to grow at all, or look weak and pale probably need brighter light. (Light in any indoor location is too low if you can't read without turning on a lamp.) Plants that thrive in northern or low light are the least tolerant of inappropriate exposures.

If any of your plants is struggling in poor or strong light where no adjustment is possible, cut down on the amount of fertilizer you give it and hold off on repotting until its roots fill the pot and protrude out the bottom drain hole. This reduced-maintenance plan will sustain your plant yet won't encourage it to grow.

This *Pelargonium* will bloom when it's moved into sun.

TYPES OF NATURAL LIGHT

Compared with that outdoors, all indoor light is weak; but what light there is varies drastically in intensity depending on the number of windows in a room and the direction they face. Of the types of interior light defined below, the brightest are direct sun, filtered light, and reflected light. Low light is always heavily filtered or reflected. Most common houseplants can survive the relative scarcity of light indoors if they are given the most suitable intensity level for their type. Here's how to identify what you've got.

Direct sun is the strongest light you can get indoors. The very brightest comes through a south-facing window that is unshaded for most of the day. Next brightest would be unobstructed morning sun through an east-facing window or afternoon light through west- and southwest-facing windows. In all such exposures, set plants at least 6 inches back from the windowpane to avoid foliage burn. Many plants grown for their flowers or fruit need a few hours of direct sun each day.

Essentially bright light, *filtered light* is softened somewhat as it shines through a sheer window covering or blinds—or perhaps through open-branched trees and shrubs growing outside the window. A translucent overhang or patio roof may also filter

Most houseplants, like the begonia 'Cleopatra' shown here, prefer bright filtered or reflected light.

light. Probably the largest number of plants thrive and bloom in bright filtered light.

Reflected light is the indirect light, cooler than direct sun, that bounces off interior surfaces. The best and brightest of this type is reflected off of light-colored walls or ceilings, illuminating the innermost spaces of a sunny room. Reflected light is generally strong enough for most foliage plants and for maintaining flowering plants that are already in bloom.

Low light inhabits the relatively dark parts of rooms, such as shadowy corners and areas unlit by windows or exposed to north-facing ones. Perhaps surprisingly, the areas to either side of a window, even just a few feet from it, receive relatively low light—only a fraction of what enters directly. Plants grown for their foliage are the best bets to place here, but of these, only a few can tolerate continuous low light; most will need a boost from an artificial source.

WAYS TO MODIFY LIGHT

You can diminish or intensify the amount of light entering a room by applying a few special tricks—and quite a few ordinary touches—to rooms that house your plants.

A reflective surface behind these plants near an east-facing window maximizes the available light.

MIRRORS. Mirrored or other reflective surfaces help distribute light throughout a room, especially behind plants that need bright light. Try to ensure that the surfaces are adjustable, so that you can move them or angle them throughout the year to catch the sun. Free-standing screens and panels are easiest to install; vertical and horizontal attachments inside and outside of windows also redirect light; south-facing ones catch the most light.

WALL COLOR. White or pale walls obviously brighten a room, but reflective wallpaper and glossy paint intensify light even more. Dark walls and draperies work the other way, generally absorbing more light than they reflect.

CLEAN SURFACES. Clean window glass and screens allow a maximum of light to penetrate indoors. Keeping plants' foliage clean, too, allows them to absorb the maximum light possible. Use a damp cloth to clean your larger plants, but avoid the commercial products that leave a glossy sheen, which may actually harm them. An easy way to clean a smaller plant is by covering the pot and soil with a plastic bag, placing it in the shower or sink, and spraying the foliage with lukewarm water. Be sure to rinse both the tops and bottoms of the leaves.

SKYLIGHTS. Windows aren't the only light source for your houseplants. Skylights brighten dim rooms with poor exposure and others darkened by exterior obstructions. Remember, not all skylights need be above interior spaces. You might consider installing an outdoor skylight in a porch roof or overhang above a window to maximize your interior light.

Keep an eye on your plants as the angle of the sun changes with the seasons through a skylight; it's easy to overlook the effect of damaging direct sunlight from above. You may need to move plants seasonally to avoid foliage burn.

GREENHOUSE WINDOWS. Although these windows that project beyond the exterior wall of a building appear to be a perfect place for houseplants, some caution is in order. Units built into south- and west-facing walls can become too bright and hot. Introduce your plants slowly to a greenhouse window, watch them closely from month to month, and be prepared to add shade if necessary. Filtered sun from a tree outside such a window may give you just the light you need.

Sunshine floods freely through skylights and greenhouse windows.

USING ARTIFICIAL LIGHT

Natural light alone is often insufficient for plants to flourish indoors. In low-light conditions, a boost from an artificial source is often the solution. When the intensity and quality of artificial light is about equal to that of natural sunlight, plants will grow quite happily, as long as they receive sufficient daily exposure. Many plants especially benefit from a combination of natural and artificial light during the winter.

TYPES OF ARTIFICIAL LIGHT

All light, whether from the sun or an electric lamp, consists of waves that appear as a spectrum of colors when passed through a prism. During the food-manufacturing process of photosynthesis, plants capture chiefly the red and blue waves of that spectrum. Cool-white fluorescent bulbs provide mostly blue light (which promotes compact foliage) and only a little red; incandescent bulbs, on the other hand, provide mainly red

light (which promotes flowering and general growth) and a little blue. Artificial light that gives a balanced combination for most plants and is closest in quality to sunlight comes from mixing 1 watt of incandescence for every 2 or 3 watts of fluorescence. (Some relatively recent lighting products will do this mixing for you, supplying the full spectrum of color for strong growth.)

Under a full-spectrum grow light, plants thrive even in a dim room that sunlight never reaches.

Generally, all plants require 15 to 20 watts of light for every square foot of their growing surface. A simple estimate of your plant's size will give you a close enough figure for determining its wattage requirement. If you use incandescent bulbs with your plants, keep in mind that most of their energy is given off as heat—often enough heat to burn a plant's foliage. Keep incandescent bulbs, therefore, at least 2 feet away from your plants.

FLUORESCENT TUBES. Given no other light source, plants can grow and flower successfully under fluorescent tubes. Fixtures having a white or foil reflector will direct the most light onto plants and waste as little as possible. Keep the light as close as you can to the foliage—as near as 4 to 6 inches (for flowering plants and compact growth) but no farther than 18 to 24 inches. Plan to leave the lights on 10 to 18 hours a day (a timer is handy) if there is no other light source. If the foliage starts to bunch together unnaturally, the plants are receiving too much light. If the plants become leggy, on the other hand, they need more light; either move them closer to the source or increase their exposure time. Other factors to consider are that more light is emitted from the center of the tube, less from the ends—and that less light is emitted as the tubes wear out. You may need several tubes if you have quite a few plants. When the lights begin to weaken, replace multiple bulbs one at a time, allowing several weeks between replacements to reduce the shock of a sudden change in light intensity.

GROW LIGHTS. A special kind of fluorescent lamp, called a grow light, provides nearly all of the wavelengths of natural light. These lamps cost more than regular fluorescent tubes and incandescent bulbs, but they can stimulate plants to bloom prolifically, produce fruit, and set seed just as they would under natural conditions. Grow lights are ideal for promoting the same type of plant growth that you would find in an outdoor garden.

When the sun hides in winter, this palm still enjoys heat and light.

IN THE SPOTLIGHT

You can use spotlights in several ways to create spectacular effects with your houseplants and supplement other light sources at the same time. Of the two common types, a reflector flood lamp disperses light, giving a less intense effect than that of a reflector spot lamp, which concentrates light. Here are some ideas to try out.

- Use overlapping beams of floodlights to increase the light level for several large plants.
- Use concentrated spots for single plants.
- Increase your winter light and heat at the same time by using several high-wattage lamps.
- Conceal lights above plants in a glass shelf unit. Some light—though of a lesser intensity—will filter down to the plants on lower shelves.

TEMPERATURE AND HUMIDITY

Luckily, most houseplants easily adjust to normal indoor temperatures, and they don't seem to mind a dip at night if the level changes less than 5 to 10 degrees. To play it safe, select plants that like the same room temperatures you do, unless you can indulge them with specialty hothouse conditions. Be aware that, as the temperature changes indoors, so does the humidity (higher temperatures bring a need for increased humidity). You'll need to give some extra care to plants native to rain forest habitats; they have difficulty in dry interiors and welcome a moisture-supplemented atmosphere.

THE COMFORT ZONE

Pampering houseplants by keeping them in a comfortable 65° to 75°F (19° to 24°C) range is really nothing more than providing conditions that most species enjoy in their native environments. You may be able to provide warmer temperatures in at least one room for finicky plants while maintaining a moderate range in the rest of the house. After all, your plants can't put on a sweater on a cool day, so they look to you to keep them comfortable.

Many plants like a change of temperature in different seasons—usually a warmer location during their active growth but a cooler one while they rest in winter. (Individual preferences are noted for each plant in "Favorite Houseplants," pages 53–110.) Most actually like the same daily temperature fluctuations that you do—about 5° to 10°F (3° to 6°C) lower at night. You can measure and record temperature changes accurately with a maximum/minimum thermometer. Knowing these precise readings helps you prevent greater variations—and undue stress for your plants—over the course of a day. Remember that, for most plants, as the temperature increases so should the humidity.

TROPICAL JUNGLE OR DRY DESERT?

Most home atmospheres offer only negligible humidity. A few plant groups, such as desert cacti and some other succulents, prefer dry air. But the majority of plants we try to grow indoors originate in tropical jungles, where the air is filled with moisture. A tropical environment is incompatible with most people's living rooms, but that's where many houseplants must live. This means two things: that plants native to a humid environment will never thrive in a dry interior, and extra humidity must be provided for certain plants.

TOP: Winter can be harsh on houseplants, damaging those left unprotected on windowsills.

BOTTOM: Succulent kalanchoe tolerates dry winter heat indoors.

Learn what temperature range your plants do best in, and then make adjustments to keep it steady. Here are a few tips and cautions for situating houseplants.

- Avoid guesswork; use a thermometer.
- Don't make drastic changes in location; move plants gradually.
- Avoid trouble spots. Air heats and dries rapidly near a stove or heat register; cold air can be trapped behind window coverings; and temperatures may fluctuate widely in bathrooms.
- Note the temperature differences between areas on the floor and closer to the ceiling. Check entry halls for chilling drafts from the doorway.

Give your plants a location checkup every month, especially after turning on your central heat or air conditioning.

A maximum/minimum thermometer automatically keeps track of fluctuating temperatures.

The foliage of these tall calla lilies acts as an umbrella in reverse: the large leaves trap water vapor as it evaporates from the shorter cinerarias *(Senecio),* increasing the humidity around them.

PROVIDING HUMIDITY

Most houseplants are tropical in origin and look their best only when provided with extra humidity. Two easy solutions are a humidity tray (top) and moist sphagnum moss sandwiched between two pots (bottom).

EASY SOLUTIONS FOR A DIFFICULT PROBLEM

In a dry atmosphere, plants lose water rapidly through their leaves in a natural process called transpiration. With excessive transpiration, leaf tips and edges shrivel and brown, buds drop, and flowering is brief—if it occurs at all. To boost plant performance and slow transpiration, you'll need to increase the humidity directly around your plants— because it's usually not convenient to increase moisture in the entire room.

Which plants need the most humidity? Generally, those with thin, delicate foliage demand a high level of atmospheric moisture. Plants with thick, leathery leaves or waxy, glossy coatings have a built-in protection against evaporation and can get by in drier air. Most houseplants thrive in relative humidity of between 40 and 60 percent. To get an exact measurement of a room's relative humidity, use a hygrometer, which you can find in garden centers specializing in houseplants.

MISTING. Though opinions vary on the value of misting, it is an easy way to create a limited humid atmosphere. If you decide to mist, always use room-temperature water and a mister that gives a very fine cloud of moisture, the best means of covering both the top and bottom of the foliage. Note that some fuzzy-leafed plants, such as African violets, should not be misted. Water drops on such leaves may cause unsightly spotting.

Misting a dieffenbachia

As you mist your plants, don't confuse misting with watering. Though plants may take in some moisture through their leaves, atmospheric moisture is no substitute for regular watering. You may want to move the plants as you mist them, to prevent water spots on furniture and windows.

USING HUMIDITY TRAYS. A good low-maintenance technique for providing extra moisture is to set plants on humidity trays. Start with a waterproof tray an inch or more in depth, large enough to hold one or several plants with some open space left around the perimeter. Fill the tray with pea gravel or small rocks; then add enough water to nearly fill the tray but not submerge the tops of the rocks. When you set the container on the pebbles, its bottom should be just above the water, so that plant roots never rot. Check the water level in the tray periodically and add more water when necessary. And always check the water level after watering, pouring off any excess drainage.

If you use a clay saucer as a humidity tray, be sure to set it on a protective pad, because clay absorbs and holds moisture that can damage the surface beneath it. For added protection, create a buffer air zone between the tray and the floor or furniture beneath it. Use a block of wood, a plant holder, or some other method to elevate the clay: air movement will help prevent damage from condensation. (See page 40 for more ideas.)

DOUBLE POTTING. Another way of maintaining humidity around a plant is by double-potting it. Choose a pot one or two sizes larger than the one holding your plant. Line the larger container with a thick layer of moist sphagnum moss and set your plant inside it. Keep the moss constantly moist so that a steady supply of water vapor surrounds the foliage.

GROUPING PLANTS. Plants themselves provide a certain amount of humidity as water evaporates from their leaves during transpiration. If you group several plants together—leaving enough room between them for free air circulation—the water vapor is caught and held by the mass of foliage. Set close together, your plants will also look lusher and take on the character of an indoor garden.

WISE WATERING

More plants fail from improper watering than from any other cause—and most often that means too much water, not too little. No two plants use water at exactly the same rate, and many factors beyond your control (such as the season of the year and the weather outside) further affect the amount of water any individual plant needs. But you can control a few factors: the type of container you select, the watering method you use, and the attention you're willing to give your plants.

KNOW YOUR PLANT

Fast-growing plants and those that bloom or bear fruit heavily need more water than do slower growers. Plants with a large total leaf surface, such as ferns, are thirstier than sparsely foliaged plants; those with soft, lush foliage usually require more water than do plants with waxy, leathery, or succulent leaves. And desert plants, of course, actually require periods of complete aridity.

KNOW YOUR POT

The type of container that holds your plant has a direct effect on the amount and frequency of watering (see pages 39–40). Because of their porosity, unglazed clay pots allow water to evaporate through the sides, which means that you need to give plants in clay more water—and check them more often.

Plastic pots are nonporous, so the potting soil inside them tends to retain moisture for longer periods than it does in a clay pot. Because the soil takes longer to dry, overwatering in plastic pots can become a real problem. Remember, as you make your rounds, that overwatering is the greatest threat to your plants' well-being. Most gardeners reserve plastic pots (or glazed clay pots) for their moisture-loving plants.

THE PROBLEM WITH SCHEDULES

If the weather—temperature, humidity, and cloud cover— could be scheduled, so could watering houseplants. Because these physical factors, combined with the indoor temperature and humidity, influence a plant's use of water, they also affect when you should water and how much you should apply. You can develop something of a routine to keep you on track, however, so long as it simply entails monitoring your plants—that is, checking for moisture rather than routinely applying it. If you must water on schedule, let it be in the morning. That's the best time to water, because moisture spattered on the foliage can evaporate by evening, discouraging the conditions in which diseases flourish.

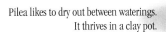

Pilea likes to dry out between waterings. It thrives in a clay pot.

TAP OR BOTTLED WATER?

Tap water is the easiest water to use, but in some locales it can seriously damage your plants. You can minimize the ill effects of chlorinated tap water by allowing it to sit uncovered in a bottle or bowl for 24 hours; the water will warm to room temperature and most of the chlorine will evaporate, making it safer for your plants.

But some tap water is simply too harmful to use on container plants. Water softener devices using ion exchangers, for example, produce water too high in sodium. Naturally hard water, on the other hand, has too high a level of alkalinity. Because most plants prefer neutral to acid conditions, you may need to give them an iron chelate supplement to offset the alkalinity of your hard water. You could try boiling hard water, which causes some of the minerals to settle out, but this is convenient only if you have a small number of plants. Using a water filter is one of the easiest ways around a water problem. In pollution-free areas, rainwater is the best type of water to use, though it may not be easy to catch! Bottled distilled water is always safe.

If you use tap water and must use it sparingly, you can find ways to recycle water that would otherwise be wasted. For instance, you can save plain, unseasoned water used in preparing and cooking vegetables to water your houseplants. But don't reuse the water that collects in the saucer under a plant; it will be too high in soluble salts from fertilizers—even organic ones—that have leached out of the soil.

HOW THIRSTY IS YOUR PLANT?

Experienced indoor gardeners have devised different ways of judging when a plant needs water. Experiment with the following methods to see which works best for you.

THE TOUCH TEST. It's generally agreed that touching is the most accurate means of judging a plant's need for water. With your finger, feel the soil surface; if the soil is still moist when you test, don't water; instead, keep checking periodically, even daily. If it's dry to a depth of ½ to 1 inch, add water. Saturate water-loving plants by adding water generously; moisten others by watering moderately. It's always good to check again after watering to see if the soil deep inside the pot is moist and not just the surface. Wait until half or more of the soil dries before refreshing plants that prefer dry conditions.

MOISTURE METER READINGS. Various gadgets for measuring the moisture content of the soil are available at nurseries and garden centers, and through mail-order catalogs. Electronic devices generate a very weak current, whose strength varies according to the amount of moisture in the soil. (In most cases, the wetter the soil, the stronger the current.) Signal types vary; most meters have a scale or dial that indicates the moisture level. Simple probes beep or change color. You may want to insert the device into different locations and soil depths in each plant. Be aware of factors that might skew the readings, such as an absence of minerals (from distilled water), the presence of salts (from soft water or fertilizer by-products), or a low battery.

OTHER INDICATORS. Drooping or wilted foliage and bone-dry soil are sure signs that a plant needs water—and fast! When you see these signs, watch what happens as you water. If the water drains right through the pot and into the saucer below, it isn't adhering to the planting mix. In such cases, allow the pot to sit in the water and absorb it from the bottom up, but never for longer than an hour. It may take several hours after watering for your plant to regain its normal perky appearance, and you may need to water a second or third time to reach the optimal moisture level. In some cases you'll have to submerge the pot in order to save your plant (see below).

Hot weather can take its toll quickly on species that depend on constantly moist soil. If you find limp foliage and stems and parched soil, give your plant a quick fix in a tub of water as shown below. This impatiens can be revived, though it may drop a few of its lower leaves.

PLANT THERAPY

Moisture-loving houseplants enjoy a soak in a tub or bucket of tepid water along with a gentle spray once in a while during a long, warm growing season. After the soaking, set pots in a protected spot to drip-dry so that surplus moisture can drain away freely.

Use the immersion method as well to water plants with excessively dry soil — when water runs down the inside of the pot as fast as you pour it in, or goes right through the mix without wetting it. (This first-aid treatment may fail to revive a plant that has already wilted, and you can expect some leaves to die on a plant that does recover.)

Immerse the pot until water just covers the rim. Use a fork or chopstick to poke holes in the soil if the water is not being absorbed readily. Soak until bubbles stop rising to the surface—no longer than 60 minutes.

Mist the foliage while the plant soaks; wash large leaves of vigorously growing—not dehydrated—plants. Allow the plant to drain for about 30 minutes before returning it to its normal location.

USING SOIL POLYMERS

Superabsorbent polymers are long-lasting gels that can absorb hundreds of times their weight in water, releasing it as the soil dries. Mixed into potting soil, gels retain both water and dissolved nutrients to keep them available near plant roots. Soil polymers let you stretch the time between waterings by curbing evaporative water loss from the soil; they also prevent wide fluctuations of moisture between waterings.

Do you need to use polymers? They're most useful for specific conditions: in drier climates or where dry spells can be expected; in soil mixes for moisture-loving plants; and when caretakers are known to be erratic! Containers that tend to dry out quickly—such as hanging baskets—can benefit from soil polymers, too.

Unfortunately, you can't just add these gels to your existing houseplants, unless you're ready to repot them. You can buy commercial potting mixes with gels already incorporated, or buy them separately and mix them in yourself. It's important to stick to the manufacturer's recommended proportions; soil that stays too wet can kill your plants.

A long-spouted watering can is handy for avoiding spills and for bypassing sensitive foliage.

WATERING TECHNIQUES

However you water your plants, you'll want to give each one the right amount of moisture for its type. Before you take a new plant home, always ask about its water needs. Too much water actually suffocates roots by depriving them of oxygen. Without air, roots rot and die. Good drainage and commonsense watering practices go hand in hand.

FROM TOP OR BOTTOM?

A lightweight watering can with a long spout puts water where you want it—on top of the soil but bypassing the foliage, in the saucer for watering from below, or directly on the foliage of plants that like the extra moisture. Be vigilant when watering from the bottom. Water can sit unnoticed in the saucer, saturating soil in the bottom of the pot and forcing roots to grow in shallow layers near the top, where the soil dries out faster.

Salts from fertilizers will accumulate in the top of the pot when you water from the bottom. You should remove them once or twice a year, either by flushing them out with several good dousings—enough to saturate the soil—or by scooping out the top inch of soil and replacing it with a fresh supply. When you water from the top, salts migrate to the bottom and are easy to flush out with deep irrigation.

BY ABSORPTION

The same double-potting technique used for supplying humidity (see page 26) can be employed for watering. Line a larger container or a cachepot with a thick layer of fibrous sphagnum moss, place a block of wood or pebbles in the bottom, and nestle your unglazed clay pot inside. You can add water either directly, to your potted plant, or indirectly, to the moss in the larger pot. The clay will absorb the moisture—though slowly—and transfer it to the potting soil. This method works best for plants that like to stay on the dry side.

TIPS ON WHEN TO WATER

Water more frequently under these conditions:

- If the container is made of unglazed clay
- When the plant is actively growing
- If the plant's roots fill the pot
- When the humidity level is lower
- When room temperature is warmer than normal

Water less frequently under these conditions:

- If the container is made of plastic or glazed clay
- When the plant is at rest
- When the humidity level is higher
- When room temperature is cooler than normal

A moisture meter will tell you at a glance the degree of dampness at the top, middle, and bottom of the root zone. More sophisticated meters than the one shown here also measure light intensity.

SOILS AND FERTILIZERS

Potting soil is a key ingredient of healthy plant growth. For most indoor gardeners, the simplest way to select houseplant soil is to buy a premixed package at a nursery or garden center. Mixes are formulated to provide excellent aeration and retain just the right amount of moisture for house-plants, allowing the excess to drain away. If you have a large collection or simply like the feel of soil between your fingers, you may want to follow one of the recipes on the facing page to make your own mix, or even devise your own unique formula with a broader combination of ingredients.

Custom-blend your own potting mix to suit each type of houseplant. Cacti and other succulents want coarse ingredients for fast drainage; moisture lovers want more organic matter.

TYPES OF POTTING MIXES

Potting soil comes in packages of various sizes, so you can purchase only as much as you need at one time or stock up and always be prepared for potting and repotting. For a while, a new mix will provide all the nutrients that a plant needs; once the plant has used these, you can replenish them with a houseplant fertilizer.

If purchasing a plastic bag of commercial potting soil isn't your idea of real gardening, gather materials of your choice and blend your own potting mix. Be sure to screen coarse materials and leave no dry, unmixed clumps. The ratios in the recipes on the facing page have proved to be ideal for most plants. Special formulations for cacti, orchids, and other specific plant groups are given under the appropriate listings in "Favorite Houseplants" (pages 53–110).

SOILLESS MIXES

Most potting mixes are not soil at all, but rather a combination of sterile organic and inorganic materials. Their primary purpose is to support the plant in its container, but a good mix will slowly release small amounts of nutrients, retain moisture, and allow for excellent drainage.

Instead of soil, most of these mixes are based on peat moss, which is lightweight and handy for large containers. Peat, however, lacks the benefit of nutrients. Some fertility is added by the manufacturer, but eventually you need to fertilize your plants on a regular basis. Because of declining sources of peat worldwide, some gardeners opt instead for mixes based on pulverized bark.

One of the best reasons for using a soilless mix is that you can easily adjust its moisture-retentive qualities by substituting one ingredient for another. The drawback is that once these materials—especially peat—dry out, they are slow to rewet, and require extra attention at watering time.

SOIL-BASED MIXES

Though garden soil makes a suitable ingredient in a potting mix, it should never be used alone, nor straight from the garden. Its chief drawback is its weight, which causes compaction in containers and inconvenience when handling large pots. Garden soil must also be sterilized before mixing it with other substances, to destroy any weed seeds and pathogens. Still, there are advantages to including it in a mix. Resident microbes digest

Continued on page 32 >

HOMEMADE BLENDS

Every potting mix should include materials that allow for water retention, drainage, and aeration. Because most houseplants need a high proportion of air around their roots, as well as residual moisture after water has drained away, a loose mixture containing some coarse material works best. Here are some standard potting soil ingredients followed by recipes for combining them.

Bark comes in graded sizes: small chips for most mixes and larger chunks for tropical plants that do not grow in soil. Commercial mixes based on bark are less expensive than peat mixes; they should contain perlite or pumice to prevent compaction over time.

Compost provides nutrients and microbial activity for plants, which is especially useful in soilless mixes. Leaf mold, aged cow manure, sawdust, fir bark, mushroom-growing medium, and other materials should be well aged and screened before use.

Peat moss varies in texture from a fine dust to long and fibrous tissue. Partly decayed sphagnum, the best type, is reddish brown, coarse, and spongy.

Sand should always be washed and be sharp or coarse in texture, like builder's sand. Mined river sand (without lime) is best; unwashed ocean sand has a dangerously high salt content.

Pumice and *lava rock* are pebbly, lightweight volcanic materials that hold moisture but more importantly prevent compaction, especially in large containers.

Perlite, which is also volcanic in origin, has been subjected to high temperatures to expand its original size. The resultant product has tiny air pockets that hold water and nutrients.

Vermiculite, a type of mica, is also expanded by heating. It absorbs and holds water longer than perlite does; use it in potting mixes for moisture-loving species.

SOIL-BASED MIX

1 part sterile soil
1 part peat moss, compost, leaf mold, or fine bark
1 part sharp sand
1 tablespoon bonemeal per 1 to 4 quarts of mix
   Fertilizer, in the proportion recommended on its label

SOILLESS MIX

1 part chopped sphagnum peat moss
1 part medium-grade vermiculite and/or compost
1 part sharp sand or perlite
1 tablespoon dolomitic limestone per 1 to 4 quarts of mix
   Fertilizer, in the proportion recommended on its label

HUMUS-RICH MIX

3 parts chopped sphagnum peat moss
3 parts compost or leaf mold
3 parts fine bark or sterile soil
2 parts sharp sand or perlite
1 tablespoon dolomitic limestone per 1 to 4 quarts of mix
   Fertilizer, in the proportion recommended on its label

Potting mixes always contain several ingredients, each selected for its role in plant growth and function. Inorganic materials that do not absorb moisture facilitate drainage best; organic materials that hold water are vital for plants that must have continual access to moisture. Shown here are (clockwise from left) premixed potting soil, vermiculite, peat moss, bonemeal, lime, perlite, bark, pumice, and washed sand.

Different types of fertilizers give different results. Experiment to see whether granular, liquid, or slow-release products are best for your plants. Apply full-, half-, or quarter-strength doses—never more than what's recommended on the label—at regular intervals from spring through fall for most houseplants.

organic matter and release a constant, though small, stream of nutrients. The clay particles in soil hold these nutrients, so they're available as needed by plant roots. And soil always has its own mineral content, which cuts down somewhat on the need for supplemental fertilizers.

STERILIZATION

Garden loam or topsoil usually contains insect pests and eggs, weed seeds, and plant disease organisms that must be excluded from an indoor mix. You can rid your soil of these contaminants by heating it, using one of the methods described below. A word of warning: Baking soil indoors gives off a nasty, lingering odor that will drive you outdoors. If you want to use the oven method, see the suggested alternatives to the kitchen stove.

THE OVEN METHOD. Mix together your nonsterile ingredients and dampen them thoroughly; spread them loosely, not more than 4 inches deep, in an ovenproof pan or plastic roasting bag. Place in a 180° to 200°F (82° to 93°C) oven and bake until the temperature throughout the soil stays at 180°F (82°C) for at least 30 minutes. (Use a meat thermometer for accuracy.) Let the soil cool completely, uncovered, in a protected area such as a garage; then store it in a plastic bag. Some gardeners choose to heat their soil only as high as 130° to 150°F (55° to 65°C), which is hot enough to destroy pathogens but spares some of the soil's beneficial microbes.

OUTDOOR COOKING. Finding an oven outdoors or even in a garage or workshop is not easy for most people, but almost everyone can find a hot plate, portable camping stove, or outdoor barbecue; these work nearly as well. The principles are the same; prepare your soil as you would for an oven treatment, but elevate your container above the alternative heat source. You may need to stir and cover the soil to help distribute the heat evenly. Be sure to use a meat thermometer for accurate measurements.

SOLARIZATION. The heat of the sun will clear pathogens from small amounts of soil spread in a clear or black plastic bag 3 to 9 inches wide. Moisten the soil just as you would for the oven method before closing the bag with an airtight fastener. Place it

in direct sun so that it receives at least 8 hours of exposure a day for about a week. Use a soil thermometer to ascertain that all of the soil is heated to between 130° and 150°F (55° and 65°C).

CHOOSING A FERTILIZER

Complete houseplant fertilizers contain three basic nutrients: nitrogen, phosphorus, and potassium (potash). The ratio is usually shown by three numbers, such as 5-10-5 or 18-20-16, printed on the label. The first number tells you the proportion of nitrogen, which stimulates leaf growth and keeps foliage a rich green. The second number indicates the proportion of phosphorus, which is necessary for sturdy cell structure, healthy root growth, and vigorous flower and fruit production. The third number gives the percentage of potassium, which fosters healthy plant development. The best fertilizers also include the secondary nutrients—calcium, magnesium, and sulfur—as well as needed micronutrients such as copper and zinc.

As long as the label indicates that the fertilizer is formulated for houseplants, you can be sure of a proper nutrient balance. A few groups of plants, such as orchids and African violets *(Saintpaulia)*, need customized fertilizers. These products are generally worth buying for superior results.

WHAT TO LOOK FOR

You can buy houseplant fertilizer as a liquid or powder, in tablets or capsules, and in fast- or slow-release forms. Before application, most need to be dissolved in or diluted with water, but some types can be scratched into the soil surface. Slow-release types allow nutrients to dissolve slowly in normal waterings over a period of time, and are applied either on or beneath the soil surface, according to package directions. Experienced indoor gardeners tend to favor liquid formulations, because of their flexibility in dilution ratios and ease of application.

FEEDING YOUR PLANTS

Though we often refer to fertilizing as a "feeding" chore, plants actually manufacture their own food through photosynthesis. Fertilizers provide the needed supplemental minerals that houseplants can't obtain any other way—nutrients that outdoor plants find in their native habitats from the soil or from the decaying organic matter that gathers in tree crotches and on the floors of forests, woodlands, and meadows. Plants growing out-of-doors can also expand their root system beyond their immediate area to seek nutrients, but a houseplant can use only the soil in its pot. Once the nutrients therein are gone, the plant is stranded. That's why you need to step in and replenish the basics by applying fertilizer.

Before fertilizing a plant, check its individual needs in "Favorite Houseplants" (pages 53–110). In addition, observe the following precautions:

- Note when your plants are undergoing a rest period. (Most rest during the winter.) Wait until they show signs of new growth before coaxing them along with nutrients.

- Never apply fertilizer in any form to dry potting soil; be sure to water your plant thoroughly first.

- Never fertilize a plant that is suffering from pests or disease; wait until it has completely recovered before encouraging it to grow.

- Never overfertilize, reasoning that if a little is good, more is better. Excess fertilizers show up as a chalky powder on the soil surface or exterior of an unglazed clay pot; they can burn foliage and even kill a plant before you identify the problem.

- Leach away accumulated fertilizer salts by watering until water runs out the drain hole; then let the plant sit for a while and water thoroughly again. Repeat this process two or three times.

ABOVE: Regular fertilizing stimulates continuous growth and normal bloom.

BELOW: This schefflera has developed rich color and a sturdy structure from a steady diet of a complete fertilizer, one containing all the needed primary, secondary, and micronutrients.

TIMING AND TECHNIQUES

Fertilizing regularly keeps plants growing steadily. For the most part, this means once every month or two, using the dilution recommended on the product label. If you use a slow- or timed-release product, you'll apply it on a regular basis according to the formulation, perhaps every 4 or 6 months. It's helpful to keep track of the dates when you applied each dose.

Some indoor gardeners believe that it's beneficial to apply fertilizer in half-strength doses more frequently (usually twice as often). This approach provides the plant with nutrients at a more continuous rate, as the timed-release types do. Other gardeners apply fertilizers in extremely light doses with each watering. Whatever method you choose, calculate carefully so that you don't overfertilize and damage your plants.

A newly purchased houseplant normally comes to you from the nursery in a well-nourished condition and shouldn't need fertilizer for 2 to 3 months—unless you completely flushed the soil when you brought it home. A newly repotted plant should not be fertilized for at least a month, to give its roots time to recover from the stress of repotting. Before you encourage it to grow with fertilizer, give it a chance to get established.

Once you've taken care of the basics—the right soil mix, light, temperature, humidity, and water—your houseplants are on their way, primed for steady growth and showplace performance.

MAINTAINING
HOUSEPLANTS

But alas, growing plants change—sometimes gradually, sometimes faster than you expect. This constant growth demands maintenance: routine grooming chores for appearances' sake, periodic repotting to give roots space to grow, and regular nipping and tucking to control size and shape. To ensure success, you'll want to choose the most suitable containers to complement your indoor plants, striking a balance between beauty and convenience.

And when your plants are so good-looking that admirers shower you with compliments, you'll be able to offer them one you've grown yourself—if you make a habit of propagating your plants along the way. Take a few cuttings or make divisions to replace flagging specimens, create gift plants, or add more of your favorites to your collection.

Although insect infestations and diseases can be a threat to any plant, they are less so to those indoors than those outdoors—still, they do occur from time to time. Giving your distressed plants immediate care is critical for returning them to good health; maintaining clean, healthy plants in the right environment is the best protection.

A potting bench in a garden shed or greenhouse keeps tools, pots, and potting mixes conveniently at hand.

uncomfortably crowded roots to a new and roomier environment. Symptoms of a pot-bound state include the following:

- Roots growing out of the drainage hole
- Roots bulging out the top of the root ball
- Foliage that looks top-heavy in proportion to the size of the pot
- Sluggish growth and smaller new leaves
- Poor water retention in the potting mix

WHEN TO REPOT

Most young plants need annual repotting to accommodate their developing root system. The time to repot is while they are vigorously growing—putting out buds, adding new foliage, and expanding in height and width—so that they can generate new root tips to replace those damaged by handling and trimming. Damaged roots absorb water slowly; they also may rot before wet soil dries out. Never repot during a resting phase, after a growth spurt, or after a long period of flowering. Wait until you see leaf buds opening and new foliage beginning to unfurl, a signal that roots are forming under the soil.

A few species need less frequent repotting, performing best when pot-bound. Check the habits of your plants in "Favorite Houseplants" (pages 53–110) before you decide that repotting is in order.

It's wise to remove and examine the root ball before you plan to move it to a larger container. Small roots that protrude from the drain hole may be wanderers rather than indicative of a clogged root ball. If what you see is mostly potting soil, put the

Continued on page 38>

TOP LEFT: Set a newly purchased plant inside a cachepot, rather than repotting immediately. Wait 1 or 2 months, until your plant adjusts to its new environment.
BELOW: Move a plant to a larger pot when its roots begin to push beyond the root ball.

POTTING AND REPOTTING

Potting pulls it all together: your houseplant, a new container, and the potting soil in which it will live. Potting is a simple yet critical part of houseplant culture, a step that keeps you in close touch with your indoor garden. As your plants grow and you move them from smaller to larger containers, you have an opportunity to give them a thorough checkup. You'll be giving crowded plants a new lease on life—a chance to stretch their legs, so to speak, and get growing again.

CHANGING POTS

Gardeners who carry home a beautiful new plant in a plain plastic container may be tempted to change pots immediately. Whether your tastes tend toward colorful glazing or traditional terra-cotta, stop for a minute and consider what's best for your plant. A move to a new container can be traumatic, and your new plant has barely adjusted to the drive home from the nursery. So it's probably a good idea to wait a bit before changing pots.

Shifting plants from one pot to another is always stressful to them in some degree, depending on the extent of disturbance to their roots. Nonetheless, doing so becomes a necessary part of houseplant care as roots reach their limits. Potting-up shifts

REPOTTING HOUSEPLANTS

Whether you work in a potting shed, on a table in a greenhouse, or at the end of your kitchen counter, you'll need some space to operate when you start repotting. Keep in mind that potting is a messy procedure. Indoors, a sheet of plastic over your work area and a dropcloth on the floor will catch spills and protect surfaces from tools and pots. The following tips will help you prepare for the operation.

POT SIZE. Never put a plant in too large a container; the new pot should have a diameter no more than 2 inches greater than the old one's, to allow ½ to 1 inch of growing space all around. In an oversize pot, the ratio of soil to roots will be too great for the roots to absorb overabundant moisture held in the soil. The resultant root rot can be a serious threat to plant health. If you want to move a newly purchased plant to a different container, choose a pot of the same size or only slightly larger.

CLEANING. Always plant into clean containers. You can wash previously used pots in soapy water with a bit of bleach added; soak them for an hour or so, scrub, and rinse well to remove any soap film. You may need to work on clay pots with a stiff-bristled brush or plastic scrubber to remove built-up salt residues from fertilizers and minerals in water.

DRAINAGE. Containers with a drain hole in the bottom are generally the safest to use, because good drainage forestalls root rot. It's not necessary to place a broken shard in the bottom of your pots, but if it's your habit to do so, there's no harm in it. It is harmful, however, to line the bottom of your pots with a layer of gravel. This takes up precious root space and in fact slows down drainage by forcing the soil to hold water longer.

MOISTURE. Water the root ball and the soil mix at least an hour before you begin. While they drain, soak any clay pots you'll be using in a tub of water. Dry porous containers draw moisture away from the soil at an unpredictable rate; presoaking them retards this water loss. Moisten your new soil mix if it's too dry. Keep a damp newspaper or sheet of plastic on hand to cover the roots and preserve their moisture in case you're interrupted.

1 Hold the stem and soil surface steady with one hand; invert the pot with the other. Strike the rim carefully against a solid surface to loosen the root ball. For hard-to-remove plants, run a sharp knife between the pot and the soil; then invert the pot, keeping the root ball intact, and remove the root ball.

2 Gently tease apart the exposed roots, loosening them with a fork or your fingers; trim the roots as needed. Remove any mossy growth from the soil surface.

3 Fill the new pot with enough soil so that the top of the old root ball sits near the top of the new pot. Center the root ball in the container and fill in around the sides with fresh mix, gently firming the soil until the sides are level with the root ball surface.

4 Smooth a trace of new soil over the top without pressing on the root ball or the plant stem. Water well, drain completely, and mist the foliage of moisture-loving plants.

plant back in its pot and wait a few months before checking again. Repot when roots grow out of the soil, but before they become tangled and wrapped around the root ball. Check for damp, brown, or mushy roots. These indicate a serious case of overwatering; trim off their rotted tips and replace all of the wet potting soil with a fresh supply.

TRIMMING ROOTS

If your plants are overdue for repotting, you may find that some roots have spiraled around or under the root ball. Loosen them as much as you can with your fingers or a fork and trim off the long, dangling sections. Try to exercise some restraint when sorting out houseplant roots; most need a lighter hand than do plants growing in the ground. If strong, fibrous roots simply refuse to budge and you can't straighten them or loosen their ends, use a sharp tool to sever and extricate a few; this will stimulate branching and allow unencumbered expansion.

Check the root ball of your houseplants once or twice a year to monitor fast-growing roots. Repot before they become as root-bound as this dracaena's. In severe cases like this, straighten all wrapped roots and trim off those too long to fit into the new pot.

If you have a plant that looks hopelessly root-bound, you may be able to untangle its matted roots by spraying them with a strong jet of water to remove most of the soil. Cut back the root mass at the bottom, but never more than one-third of the total root ball. Prune off up to one-third of the foliage as well, to prevent wilting and water loss, and wait for new growth to appear before resuming normal watering and fertilizing. After repotting, mist and cover your plant loosely with a clear plastic bag for at least a week or two to help hold in humidity. This trimming procedure rejuvenates roots but causes considerable stress as well; your plant will need a long period of rest and recovery.

Some plants are more sensitive than others to root disturbance. Care guidelines for palms and gardenias, for example, recommend treating their roots gently or not disturbing them at all. In such cases, don't worry about straightening or trimming; just fill in fresh soil around the roots. Timely repotting is the best approach with these plants.

Before repotting, trim off any long roots that spiral under the root ball.

TOP DRESSING

Though several species of houseplants— common geraniums *(Pelargonium)*, Kaffir lily *(Clivia miniata)*, and some other bulblike plants—seem to enjoy being pot-bound, they also welcome a layer of fresh soil or compost over the top of their roots. To top-dress these plants, spoon or brush away the upper quarter to third of the soil, taking care not to damage any roots. Discard this soil and replace it with the same type of soil mix originally used. You may want to blend in a timed-release fertilizer or compost for an extra boost.

Over time, soil at the top of the pot loses fertility and often accumulates salts. Replace it with a fresh supply.

CONTAINERS GALORE

The vast array of plants tempting you in the nursery is surpassed only by the number of containers available. A myriad of choices abounds: clay or plastic pots and saucers, cachepots and baskets, wicks and reservoirs—all useful to indoor gardeners for holding sculptural succulents, wisps of greenery, lavish bloomers, or a dramatic tree. Take your time when selecting, to determine what best suits your plant, its surroundings, and your own budget and taste.

POTS FOR STYLE AND FUNCTION

Veteran indoor gardeners who value plants more than pots look for function before form. They know that long-lasting plant health depends on the size and type of pot as well as on proper care. Yet any plant enthusiast can fall for a dynamite decorative container before ever selecting a plant to put in it. Each container has a visual impact, whether formal or whimsical, and works with the plant to alter the environment in your home.

As you look for a pot, keep a few points in mind. First, containers with drainage are generally a wiser choice. Plant care gets tricky in a drainless pot. Second, purchase a drip saucer when you buy the pot, not later; that's when size and compatibility of style are easiest to judge. Third, choose the container that best suits your plant's present size. Small plants with small root systems don't do well in large containers. As plants grow, however, they may need a consecutively larger pot each year.

WORKING WITH CLAY

Always popular, classic terra-cotta or clay pots are inexpensive and easy to find. These pots are porous: they absorb moisture and permit beneficial air circulation. They're great for beginning gardeners, because it's difficult—though not impossible—to overwater a plant in a clay pot. Clay also makes it easy to notice excess mineral salts that form a white crust on the outside of the pot. This indicates that you may be overfertilizing; at the least, it's a reminder to flush those salts away from plant roots.

Orchids and decorative pots make an artistic statement in this setting.

Clay pots have evolved from one basic flowerpot design to a wide assortment of sizes and shapes, from square to rectangular to cylindrical, from tiny 2-inch midgets to oversize giants that can be moved only with heavy equipment. Standard pots have a height equal to their width at the rim; azalea pots are three-quarters as deep as their width, and bulb pots are half as deep as they are wide. The shallower designs are best for shallow-rooted species, such as African violets and other gesneriads, prayer plants *(Maranta)*, and begonias. Clay's earthy color (usually reddish orange, though sometimes available in shades of brown or gray) blends well with most furniture styles and doesn't overshadow the plant.

PLASTIC AND FIBERGLASS

Easy to clean, inexpensive to buy, and light in weight, plastic containers come in a wide variety of colors, shapes, and sizes. Some are drab and utilitarian but easy to camouflage; others are bright and stylish. All are more durable than clay and less likely to crack if bumped or

Clay and plastic pots don't have to be plain and utilitarian. Decorative new designs are especially appealing when holding nonblooming foliage plants such as this Chinese evergreen *(Aglaonema)*.

dropped. As handy as plastic pots are, their greatest asset is their worst liability: they hold in moisture. Plastic doesn't "breathe" as clay does, so water can't evaporate through the pot's sides. The resulting lack of air circulation and potential for excess moisture too often spell trouble from overwatering, which blocks out air and causes root degeneration. Many gardeners prefer to put only moisture-loving plants tolerant of dampness in plastic containers and to use clay for everything else. If you do use plastic, remove the root ball every few months at first to check up on the well-being of the roots until you achieve the right balance as you water.

Also nonporous and similar to plastic in weight and durability, fiberglass pots are molded and colored to look like stone or clay. You may have to search them out in specialty mail-order catalogs or nurseries. Most are pricey but make striking containers for large plants in designer settings, without the weight of the pots they mimic.

DECORATIVE DRAINLESS CONTAINERS

A container may be made of almost anything; in fact, some of the most eye-catching ones weren't originally intended for plants at all. An old teapot, a silver bowl, a decorative tin can—the candidates are limited only by your imagination.

Glazed ceramic pots offer grander ornamentation than their clay or plastic counterparts. Though more decorative, they're also much more expensive—but their rich colors and vivid patterns may make the cost worthwhile. Like plastic pots, glazed containers are nonporous and may present watering problems for a beginner. If you find the perfect one for your decor, consider using it as a cachepot or jardiniere: nestle a less attractive pot inside, as you would inside a basket.

SELF-WATERING POTS

For the frequent traveler or the gardener who sometimes leaves plants untended, self-watering systems are like an automatic green thumb, always there with water and dilute fertilizer. Most operate on the principle of capillary action, which draws water up from a refillable reservoir until the soil becomes evenly moist. Several types are sold, from simple wicks in saucers to more sophisticated designs employing a sensor that regulates water intake. As the potting soil dries out, water is pulled in and then stops, in an ongoing wet/dry cycle. Depending on the size of the reservoir and ambient conditions, self-watering pots can keep soil moist for 1 to 4 weeks.

A houseplant collection in self-watering pots makes indoor gardening a breeze.

These nifty helpers are ideal for supplying constant moisture to a whole group of plants of various species that need periods of heavy watering or that should never dry out. Fuzzy-leafed kinds like African violets, which benefit from drawing moisture from the bottom of the pot, as well as indoor trees that need frequent watering also thrive in self-watering pots. Plants that prefer periodic dry spells—such as cyclamen, cacti, and succulents—do not do well in these pots, nor do plants with aggressive root systems.

OTHER OPTIONS

If your plant needs extra air around its roots, you might consider planting it in a paper pulp container, a moss-lined wire basket, or a pot with pierced or slotted sides (the latter are designed especially for orchids). Soil in these containers won't stay soggy after watering, and harmful salts don't build up around the roots; instead, they filter out through the walls. This porosity does mean that the soil can dry out quickly, so you'll need to water frequently—often more than once a day in warm temperatures.

OFF THE FLOOR

One way to promote air circulation and simultaneously prevent water stains on floors is to raise your containers on legs or some other support. Put wood blocks, stands on casters, or purchased decorative "pot feet" beneath pots. Use terracotta pot feet only on ceramic tile floors, because they also conduct moisture. Providing waterproof drip trays or saucers is an even more effective way to keep water stains off floors. (Be sure to empty the saucers, though, so the soil doesn't stay soggy.) These trivets and pot feet are available at nurseries and garden centers. To make wooden supports for oversize pots, use wood screws to fasten strips of 1- by 2-inch lumber together in a triangle, square, or rectangle large enough to hold a pot and saucer.

SHAPING AND GROOMING

Routine grooming goes a long way to ensure healthier plants. Each species has its own specific needs, but all require regular cleaning, just as your furniture does. And nearly every plant with multiple stems needs shaping and trimming now and then. Gentle washing and showers take the place of natural rainfall; pinching keeps plants full; trimming and adding support control size and shape, enhancing your plants aesthetically as they age.

Surroundings—the height of a ceiling, the surface area of a tabletop, the dimensions of a room—tend to dictate the optimal size for your houseplants. Careful pinching and periodic pruning are the simplest and safest ways to keep many plants in scale with their environment. Root pruning helps you maintain a favorite plant in the same pot for many years. But if a houseplant has grown too leggy (tall and spindly, with sparse foliage), unwieldy, or misshapen, even drastic pruning probably won't do much good. It's best to simply discard such a plant and start over.

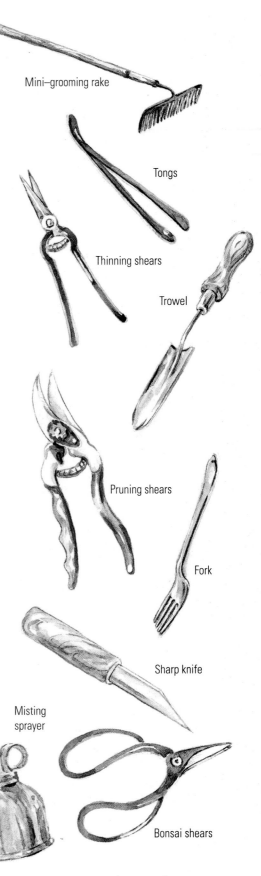

Mini–grooming rake

Tongs

Thinning shears

Trowel

Pruning shears

Fork

Sharp knife

Misting sprayer

Bonsai shears

GROOMING FOR HEALTH

It takes a light touch when cleaning plants to avoid damaging tender foliage.

Plants stay healthier when clean foliage allows them to absorb optimal amounts of light during photosynthesis. It's a fairly easy grooming chore, especially on large plants, to hand-wash large leaves with plain water and a damp cloth or soft sponge. Commercial products that give foliage a glossy sheen aren't as wonderful as the initial effect they create; in fact, they can harm some plants by clogging their pores. You can clean a smaller plant by covering just the pot with a garbage bag, placing it in the shower or sink, and spraying the foliage with lukewarm water (use only unsoftened water). Be sure to rinse both tops and bottoms of the leaves and let your plant drain well after its shower. In warm weather, a gentle outdoor spray with a hose works well, so long as you don't expose your plants to harsh sun.

TOOLS AND TECHNIQUES

Though the average outdoor gardener may collect a full battery of pruning tools, a houseplant caretaker needs only a few for trimming and grooming. You don't even have to buy—and you'll never misplace—the two pruning tools most often used: your thumb and forefinger. These handle most pruning jobs on soft-stemmed plants. Rely on a sharp knife, scissors, or small hand pruners for cutting tougher stems. A few plants, such as euphorbias and ficus, have a milky sap that may cause dermatitis; it's best to wear gloves or use a hand tool when trimming them.

PINCHING FOR FULLNESS

Like preventive medicine, proper pinching as plants grow prevents the need for more radical treatment later on. Pinching stops growth in one direction and redirects it in another. You can easily control the fast-growing stems of species like coleus *(Solenostemon)* and inch plant *(Callisia)* by nipping off the tips. This promotes denser branching and leafiness along the stems.

Effective pinching leaves no stub, but rather removes the entire stem just above a node—each point where a leaf is attached. Removing this top growth forces lower side buds to form new leaves and branches. The result is a fuller, well-shaped plant (see the illustration at left). To get the densest foliage, start pinching while stems are short to encourage the formation of side shoots close to the plant's center. Repeat pinching as often as necessary during your plant's growing season.

As blossoms on a flowering plant fade, pinch them off, too. "Deadheading" spent blossoms keeps your plant neat and tidy and diverts its energy from seed production. The result will be a longer blooming period and a stronger plant.

SELECTIVE PRUNING

Top pruning—or cutting back—removes more of the plant than pinching does. This procedure restores a plant's shape by shortening leggy stems or branches grown awry. As you would in pinching, make cuts above a node, where a branch, leaf, or set of leaves is attached to the stem. It's important to make well-placed cuts for two reasons: plants can more quickly seal over wounds made at a node, and dormant buds are waiting to open at the node. As a new bud unfolds on a stem tip, that shoot becomes the new "leader" as it attempts to reestablish the plant's height. When several stems compete to be leaders in several directions, growth becomes fuller. Your plants will respond best and fastest if you do this kind of pruning at the beginning of their growing season.

If you decide to remove a whole branch to reduce the size of a large plant, use sharp pruning shears and cut as close as possible to the main stem or all the way to the base. Woody shrubs and flowering plants like gardenias and hibiscus need this kind of heavy pruning to maintain a compact shape. Removing the oldest stems helps them produce new ones low on the plant year after year.

ROOT PRUNING

At some point, you'll need to start pruning roots as well as top growth as part of your annual plant-grooming exercise. This usually begins when you choose to stop moving a plant up to a larger pot size, whether or not it has reached its ultimate size. Because your plant's root system continues to expand, you'll need to prune those roots so they don't fill the pot completely. You may be able to schedule this operation for every 2 or 3 years on mature plants; check younger ones annually.

To root-prune a plant, set up a spacious work area and remove the plant from its pot. The soil should be neither bone-dry nor so moist that the root ball crumbles completely. Loosen the soil around the container walls with a knife

Pinch plants on all sides—at the top and at the tips of side branches—to keep growth full and even.

Use sharp scissors when pruning off damaged foliage or cutting back long stems.

Plants that stay in the same container need repotting and root pruning every 1 to 3 years.

and lay the pot on its side. Tap around the rim with a rubber mallet and pull the plant free, grasping the root ball rather than the plant to avoid damaging its stems.

Use the same techniques as you would to repot a root-bound plant (see "Trimming Roots," page 38): loosen any wrapped or twisted roots, and then shake off the outer soil and trim the roots so they'll be surrounded by an inch of fresh soil on all sides after you replace the root ball. Never prune away more than one-third of the total volume, and always use a sharp tool that makes clean cuts. Keep the humidity level high around your plant after repotting, to compensate for water loss through the foliage while new roots form.

FRESHENING THE POT

Even if you're not changing pot size, after its annual grooming your plant will benefit from having a clean container for its next growth spurt. Take time to scrub both the inside and outside before you repot, to destroy molds and remove salts. Use a stiff brush and a hot but mild solution of household bleach; rinse well. Add fresh potting mix—the same type that's in the root ball—when you replace the plant in the pot.

LENDING SUPPORT

All weak-stemmed plants need help to look attractive and grow upright; otherwise, they'll droop and trail, an advantage only if you want a hanging plant. You can transform climbers of any size into interesting sculptural shapes or architectural features by giving them a shapely support: for instance, a moss-covered pole, a wooden trellis, or molded metal. You'll find many functional designs that are quite attractive on their own.

To support trees or tall, treelike plants, use a large-diameter bamboo stake or wooden pole and a stout yet pliant material for ties. Place the stake directly in the pot at planting time for the least disturbance to the roots. Check the size of your container: it should be large enough to hold the stake yet allow ample space for root development, and it should be weighty enough so that it doesn't become top-heavy under a mass of foliage. Tie the stem to its support, using a figure-eight loop that allows your plant some movement. To support small plants, use a thin bamboo stake or a chopstick and a soft, flexible tie. Never tie plants with wire or any other material that might cut into a stem.

A few plants, such as impatiens, chrysanthemum, aluminum plant *(Pilea),* and some ferns, look best if most or all of their growth is supported above a circular grid or hoop thrust into the soil mix on "legs." You can purchase preformed metal supports or make your own adjustable ones by looping twine—green is least noticeable—around each of three or four small stakes equally spaced around the inside edges of a pot.

Begin training plants while they're young and flexible. Take care not to break their stems as you tie them, or you may lose the leader you're trying to train. Figure-eight ties are best, because they allow room for expansion without strangulation. You'll have the best success if you tie all climbing plants to get them started, including those such as ivy *(Hedera)* and creeping fig *(Ficus pumila)* that have their own twining tendrils or gripping aerial roots.

A moss-covered pole suits climbing plants doubly well: it lends support and holds moisture for aerial roots.

PROPAGATING HOUSEPLANTS

Propagating your own houseplants is a different kind of gardening activity than routine care. It's an exciting challenge that many plant lovers relish and is by far the least expensive way of acquiring new plants. Don't be disappointed if not all your prospects live to tell the tale; many variables are involved, and a 100-percent success rate is rare. Still, most plants respond readily, which makes propagation immensely rewarding. With new specimens at the ready, you'll have plenty of gift plants to hand out to admirers and ample replacements for declining favorites in your own collection.

If you like the varieties you already have, start duplicating them with one of the techniques discussed here: rooting offsets and plantlets, separating and dividing, taking leaf and stem cuttings, and layering. Except for sowing seeds, which can take years and end unpredictably, all methods of starting new plants are known as vegetative propagation—that is, by using a part of one plant, you create another separate but identical one. The method you use depends on the type of plant and how much time you want to devote to the process. For best success, coddle your new plants for a while after they're on their own to protect them from too-bright light and too-frequent watering. Wait until you see some new growth before starting light doses of fertilizer.

ROOTING OFFSETS AND PLANTLETS

Small offsets and plantlets appear as outgrowths or appendages above the soil on established plants of several genera. You'll find them attached to the base of the parent plant, on a leaf, or at the end of a stem or runner—perhaps with some roots attached, all ready for planting. Hen and chicks *(Echeveria* and *Sempervivum),* strawberry begonia *(Saxifraga stolonifera),* and spider

Plantlets form atop the fronds of a mother fern.

plant *(Chlorophytum)* all commonly form plantlets. Look for them also at the base of a piggyback *(Tolmiea)* leaf and on the fronds of a mother fern *(Asplenium bulbiferum).* The miniatures need only come in contact with moist potting soil to form more extensive roots and grow into new, full-size houseplants.

Baby plantlets stay attached to the parent spider plant until they have formed their own root mass.

The easiest method of rooting is to place the plantlet, still attached to the parent plant, in a container filled with moist potting soil. If necessary, use a partially opened paper clip to keep the base of the plantlet in contact with constantly moist but never soggy soil. As new growth appears on the plantlet, check for roots below the soil. When the offspring's root mass is sufficient, sever the stem connecting it with the parent plant at a point close to the plantlet.

To divide a sansevieria, cut through its rhizomes.

SEPARATING AND DIVIDING

No propagation method is easier than separating clumps of rooted offsets from around the base of a plant. Most bromeliads and many desert cacti, for instance, produce several 3- to 4-inch small plants (sometimes called pups) around their base after flowering. You can pull or cut them away as soon as they're well rooted and pot them up. Separating clumps on mother plants, such as African violets and many succulents, leaves them more attractive in addition to multiplying your supply of plants.

Dividing plants that expand at their crown—where stems and roots join—calls for a heavier hand and a sharp knife. Some clumps, like those of asparagus fern, are so tough that you may need a cleaver; others, like mother-in-law's tongue *(Sansevieria),* are more easily cut apart. Just as you would do when dividing outdoor perennials, place the root ball on a flat surface and shake or brush away enough soil to allow you to work freely and quickly, keeping plant stress to a minimum. Cut cleanly down through the crown, leaving a minimum of two or three stems in each division. Discard any dead or diseased sections and trim away long, trailing roots.

Plants that grow from rhizomes below the soil are sometimes loosely intertwined in groups or firmly connected by fleshy roots. Pull the rhizomes apart if you can—they separate easily on peace lily *(Spathiphyllum)*—or cut through more resistant sections, such as you'll find in sympodial orchids. Always leave three or more shoots in each division. Rhizomatous plants generally maintain their vigor readily when you divide them, because they have access to nutrients in their rhizome storehouse. Still, a little tender care will go a long way as they put down new roots. For example, young kohlerias and other gesneriads will reward you with more robust plants in a shorter time if you enclose them in glass or plastic and keep the humidity high while they get established.

TAKING LEAF AND STEM CUTTINGS

In order to root cuttings, you'll need a medium that holds moisture easily yet is well aerated. Choose perlite, vermiculite, coarse sand, a half-perlite and half-sand mixture, or standard indoor potting soil combined with enough perlite to lighten its texture. Whatever medium you decide on, be sure your mix is sterilized to prevent damage from fungal disease (see page 32). If your first attempts produce only spotty success, adjust the mix. Here are some tips for success with this propagative technique.

- Root cuttings in spring or early summer, or whenever your plant's natural growth period occurs.

- Dip your cuttings in a rooting hormone to stimulate root formation if you find that your plant is hard to root. Nurseries carry these hormones in both liquid and powder forms.

- Keep the rooting medium moist (like a squeezed-out sponge) but not soggy. When cuttings produce new growth, transplant them into a more suitable potting mix.

- Enclose your cuttings in a plastic bag for 2 to 3 months or until you see new growth. Check the moisture level and provide air by opening the bag from time to time.

- Add bottom heat if the temperature is much below 65°F/19°C. At lower temperatures, rooting is slow and rot is common.

LEAVES

A number of fleshy-leafed plants, such as peperomia *(P. argyreia, P. caperata,* and *P. griseo-argentea),* African violet *(Saintpaulia),* gloxinia *(Sinningia),* and rex begonia, will root successfully from a leaf or portion of a leaf. One method is to remove a vigorous, mature leaf with its complete petiole (leaf stem) attached. Use a pencil or small stick to poke a hole in the rooting medium and insert about three-fourths of the petiole. Firm the rooting medium gently, so that the leaf remains vertical. These leaves sometimes root successfully in water alone, when only the petiole is immersed.

A second method of leaf propagation is to cut through the veins on the underside of a leaf (see the illustration on page 46). Lay the cut side down on a moist rooting medium; sprouts will appear along the cut veins and roots will grow underneath. Finally, peperomia, sansevieria, and rex begonia all root easily from a leaf cut in half horizontally with the broader, bottom end inserted in a rooting medium. When preparing cut sections of a sansevieria leaf, label the top with a marking pen so you know which end should be up when you put it in the rooting medium.

TOP: This root-bound orchid is ready to divide into two or three sections.

BOTTOM: Trim off any damaged roots and place each section in a new or freshly scrubbed pot.

A loose plastic covering over leaf cuttings slows down evaporative water loss and speeds rooting.

It takes 2 or 3 and sometimes up to 6 months before sprouts appear on leaf cuttings. They root fastest when you keep them in bright light and provide a humid atmosphere. Contrive a minigreenhouse using a plastic bag, transparent storage box, or glass bowl if you don't have a commercial humidity dome; however, do not cover leaf cuttings of succulent plants like sansevieria in this fashion.

STEMS

To propagate plants like coleus *(Solenostemon)*, aluminum plant *(Pilea)*, and hoya, take tip cuttings. Remove the top 4 inches of a vegetative stem (one without flowers) by slicing it with a sharp knife just below a leaf. Remove the lower leaves so none sits inside the rooting medium. Some plants, like ivy *(Hedera)* and wandering Jew *(Tradescantia)*, are even easier to propagate. Simply place a stem in a glass of water and plant it when you see roots 1 to 2 inches long. Other plants such as orchid cacti *(Epiphyllum)* form small "adventitious" roots at their nodes as the stems grow; these readily form new plants when you take cuttings.

When plants like dieffenbachia and dracaena develop tall, gangly stems and drop their lower leaves, you can rejuvenate them in one of two ways. Either layer the stem below the foliage (see "Air Layering," at right) or take stem cuttings to start over with a new plant. In the latter procedure, you remove short lengths of older sections having at least two nodes—circular ridges, with or without leaves attached, that conceal dormant buds. Press these cuttings horizontally into the surface of a moist rooting medium, so that good contact is made with the bottom half of each section.

ABOVE, TOP TO BOTTOM: A begonia leaf cutting; a bougainvillea stem cutting dipped in rooting hormone; a geranium cutting ready to root in a soil mix

BELOW: Place dracaena stem cuttings horizontally on the soil. Each small stem section will yield at least one new plant.

LEAF CUTTING

STEM CUTTINGS

LAYERING

In layering, a branch is rooted while it is still attached to a plant. This propagation technique tends to be slow, but it is useful for some hard-to-root plants.

GROUND LAYERING

With more space around them, outdoor plants are fairly easy to layer in the ground. Layering potted plants becomes a little awkward, because there's less soil area to work with. Also, you have to remove them from display during the time it takes them to root, which can take many weeks. But several houseplants—ivy, fittonia, and philodendron—root quickly when their flexible stems are buried in a smaller pot or tray of moist rooting medium. It helps to cut halfway through the stem and to put a tiny pebble in the cut to hold it open slightly before pinning it down. You may need to tie the stem's tip to a small stake to hold it upright.

AIR LAYERING

The principle of air layering is the same as that of ground layering; the difference is that air layering is used for branches higher up on a plant. It works well in rejuvenating large plants—such as codiaeum, dracaena, and ficus—that naturally develop height and legginess over the years.

Begin air layering below a node where you want the new roots to start. Choose a spot on the previous year's growth that has hardened somewhat; make an upward slanting cut (inserting a matchstick to keep it open) or remove a ring of bark. Dust the cut or peeled stem with rooting hormone and encase it in damp sphagnum moss. Tie a plastic wrapping around the moss and fasten it securely at the top and bottom—above and below the cut—so that moisture won't escape. It's a good idea to check every week or so at first, to be sure that the moss stays moist. It usually takes several months before roots form.

Air-layering a ficus

When you see roots or feel them pushing against the plastic, sever the newly rooted stem from the mother plant. At this time it is usually wise to halve the number of leaves, to prevent excessive loss of moisture through transpiration while the newly independent plant establishes itself. If no roots form, the branch will callus where it was cut, and you can try again in another spot.

KEEPING PLANTS HEALTHY

Discovering an ailing houseplant is always a blow. What's worse is realizing that your own improper care is the likely culprit. Most houseplant problems can, in fact, be traced to cultural causes: poor light, over- or underwatering, over- or underfertilizing, the wrong temperature and humidity, or an unsuitable potting mix. Determining which of these conditions is to blame and how much of an adjustment you need to make adds to the puzzle; often it's a combination of factors that causes a plant to fail.

TOP: Overwatered dieffenbachia
BOTTOM: Chlorosis on gardenia

TOP: Aphids on geranium
BOTTOM: Scales on a palm frond

The charts in this section feature the most common houseplant problems. They'll help you pinpoint causes and choose remedial methods of control. When you detect any sign of distress, treat it as a cry for help; prompt attention with the least toxic treatment available is always the best response. You may need to review the specific care advice in "Favorite Houseplants" (pages 53–110) to get your plant back on track.

SIGNS OF TROUBLE

A commonsense approach is the best way to tackle houseplant troubles. Try, first of all, to develop a sharp eye for anything that seems abnormal. Then, as problems show up, check your growing conditions to be sure that your plant is getting what it needs to thrive.

Fluoride injury

And know your plants. Some are tough and cheerfully survive abuse; others are particularly sensitive and react to any kind of change, even a simple move from one room to another. Unless you have an abundant store of patience, it may be wise to avoid buying the touchy ones in the first place and rely on the more durable species.

DIAGNOSING AILMENTS

A thorough annual checkup at repotting time will meet the minimum needs of your houseplants, but it's a good idea to set up a more frequent routine for close observation. Up-close monthly or weekly inspections should reveal problem situations and tell you if you need to take action. What should you look for? Know what your plant should look like in its healthiest condition and compare that with any changes.

Scrutinize the foliage for discoloration along leaf margins, tips, or centers; notice unusual spots, blotches, or mottling.

Evaluate changes in texture as well as color. Compare the appearance of new growth to that of mature foliage; notice any leaf distortion, stunting, or wilting.

Note changes in stem growth, such as abnormal bumps or notches. Look for discoloration (brown areas) near the stem's base, and don't overlook exaggerated growth between leaves.

If possible, take the root ball out of the pot to check the roots. Look for damaged sections, soft and mushy pieces, or white, fuzzy patches.

When diagnosing a problem, start by eliminating possible causes of symptoms one by one to arrive at the most likely source of trouble. And try to look beyond the obvious for as many clues as you can find. The presence of ants, for instance, may be troubling, but the real problem is more likely an infestation of sucking insects that excrete the honeydew that attracts ants. It may take a while to return your plants to good health, because some species grow so slowly that the symptoms may not disappear even after the problem is solved. Yellowed leaves, for example, will not green up again after you fix a watering problem, but new growth will emerge bright green.

CULTURAL PROBLEMS

PROBLEM	PROBABLE CAUSE	REMEDY
Yellowing leaves	Too little or too much light. Too little or too much fertilizer. High temperatures, especially at night. Too much water. High lime content in potting mix. (Be aware that older leaves may yellow and drop naturally.)	Move plant into filtered or reflected light. Fertilize more frequently, or use a lower dosage if you're already fertilizing frequently. Find a cooler location. Improve drainage and do not allow water to sit in saucer; probe soil for moisture before watering. Repot annually with suitable soil mix.
Browning leaf tips and leaf margins	Too much or too little water. High salt concentration in water. Too much fertilizer. Insufficient humidity. Too much sun or heat. Drafty location. Foliar bruising from rough handling or high-traffic location.	Improve drainage and do not allow water to sit in saucer; probe soil for moisture before watering. If soil dries quickly, water frequently, replant into larger pot, or add polymers or vermiculite to hold moisture. Leach out fertilizer salts and use only salt-free (not softened) water. Reduce fertilizer dosage. Increase humidity. Move plant to a more protected location.
Brown or yellow spots or blotches on leaves	Too much water. Too much direct sun. Too hot or too drafty a location.	Water less frequently and improve drainage. Move plant into filtered or bright reflected light. (Plants moved from low light into direct sun are most quickly affected.) Adjust artificial light. Find a more suitable location.
Dry and brittle leaves; leaves curled under	Underwatering. Insufficient humidity. Too much or too little heat.	Review watering practices. Raise humidity by regular misting or using a humidity tray. Move plant to warmer or cooler location.
Leaf drop	Over- or underwatering. Too much sun. Too much fertilizer. Low humidity. Drafty location. Lower leaves may drop if light is too low or temperature changes abruptly. Annual leaf drop is normal on some plants, such as weeping fig (Ficus benjamina).	Review all aspects of plant care. Move plant to a more suitable location. New leaves are unlikely to replace dropped ones. If plant does not regain health or loses its attractive appearance, replace it.
Wilting	Too much or too little water. Too much sun or heat. Poor growing location.	Review watering practices and check root health; trim rotted roots and repot in fresh soil. Water dry soil (plant will perk up but may lose some leaves if wilting occurs repeatedly). Move plant out of direct sun, high heat, or drafty location.
Leggy growth or stems bent toward light	Too little light.	Pinch back long stems. Move plant to brighter light; if light is artificial, increase wattage or move lamps closer to plant.
Small, pale new growth	Too little light. Too little fertilizer.	Move plant to brighter light; if light is artificial, increase wattage or move lamps closer to plant. Fertilize regularly throughout growth period.
Failure to bloom	Temperatures too high during plant's rest season. Inadequate light during growth season.	Reduce temperature and exposure to light during plant's dormancy, especially at night. During active growth, gradually move plant into brighter light or direct sun, depending on species.
Flower bud drop	Too little light or too much direct sun. Improper watering. Insufficient humidity or fertilizer. Temperature too low or too erratic after buds form.	Adjust plant's exposure to light. Review watering practices. Raise humidity or augment fertilizer applications. Move plant to location with more even temperature range.

PESTS AND DISEASES

Indoor pests are so small—some almost microscopic—that you may not notice the little marauders until your plant takes an alarming turn for the worse. Plant diseases, on the other hand, show more noticeable symptoms, though disease is less common and attacks only a few susceptible plants. Routine inspections should enable you to control both kinds of problems before serious damage is done.

RECOGNIZING INTRUDERS

Insects do show up now and again—more often if unscreened windows and doors are frequently open. They may also piggyback inside on plants that have spent the summer out-of-doors. A thorough examination before returning these plants indoors helps, but it's a good idea to keep an eye out for interlopers for another week or two. The best defense is always a vigorous plant, whether indoors or out—the more robust its health, the greater its resistance to any pest or disease.

One way to identify pests is by the damage they do. Chewed leaves while plants are outside may reflect the activities of weevils, snails, or slugs. Indoors, you may find mottling or disfigured foliage from sucking or rasping pests: scale, aphids, mealybugs, spider mites, and thrips.

You'll need a magnifying glass to identify a few of these pests. It takes especially close scrutiny to find mites and thrips; aphids, whiteflies, mealybugs, and scale are easier to distinguish because of their size, color, or tendency to cluster in colonies. If you suspect any of them, don't wait for a final identification. Isolate all infested plants immediately and keep them in quarantine for 1 to 3 weeks or until the problem is cleared up. Do identify any pest, however, before you attempt a chemical treatment. Pesticides are formulated to control specific insects.

You'll have little difficulty recognizing snails and slugs or caterpillars, earwigs, and other larger insects if they attack your plants, but these rarely do unless the plants are outside or on porches or patios for a long visit. Check your plants periodically for chewed stems and leaves; also look for other signs such as fecal droppings and tunnels in leaf interiors. Simply pick off the pests and badly damaged leaves when you see them, reserving heavier-handed treatments for severe problems.

TOP: Spider mites on impatiens
MIDDLE: Greenhouse whiteflies
BOTTOM: Stem rot on begonia

IDENTIFYING DISEASES

Few diseases attack houseplants; those that do oftentimes arise from poor cultural care—mostly, this means overwatering or using unsterilized soil. Viral infections may cause disfiguring yellowish spots, streaks, or mottling; various bacteria also cause leaf spots, watery blotches, and depressions on foliage. Fungal problems are more common—spores are easily airborne, just waiting for the ideal combination of host plant, temperature, and moisture before they settle in. If you find soft stem bases, soft or spongy roots, or either white or black molds, suspect a fungal infection. Always cut off and destroy diseased portions of any plant to forestall spreading.

If you suit environmental conditions to your plant's health rather than to the pathogen, you will have few if any disease problems. In some cases, simply changing a few care routines, such as watering less or lowering the temperature or humidity, means the difference between persistent problems and carefree indoor gardening. Long-term disease control almost always requires changing the growing environment.

Root rot on jade tree

LINES OF DEFENSE

There are two ways to fight pests. You can take the direct approach—which demands a little time and perseverance—and simply remove them by hand or wash them off under running water from a hose or faucet. (Be sure to clean the leaf undersides as well; many

Treat scale insects as shown on this staghorn fern, by dipping cotton in denatured alcohol and daubing the leaves.

Spot-treating minor mealybug infestations is the best approach, especially on cacti and other succulents such as the lithops shown here.

insect pests like to hide there.) Or you can use a pesticide. Many types of products—from soap sprays to toxic chemicals—are effective controls, though few are completely beneficial for your plant. The drawbacks to pesticide use are twofold: the cure may harm the plant as much as it does the pest, and the product may have a serious impact on human health and the larger environment.

Though removing damaged plant parts and changing the growing environment are often the most effective and always the least toxic approach to controlling both pests and diseases, some gardeners automatically reach for a spray. If you choose to spray, it's best to work in a spacious area outside. There you can be sure of covering all leaf surfaces, top and bottom, without worrying about damaging nearby furnishings. This also ensures that any spray residue can disperse in the open air. Maintain the recommended distance between the spray canister and the plant's foliage; sprays may burn plants if applied too closely. Ready-mixed spray containers of insecticide and fungicide offer the most practical option for houseplants. These have been diluted to the correct ratio and are easy to apply to the affected plant.

Always explicitly follow the directions printed on the label of any chemical control. If you have spray materials on hand, check to see that the expiration date has not passed and that the insecticide or fungicide is effective on the specific pest or disease attacking your plant. Also, confirm that it's recommended for use on houseplants—and for your particular plant. Some delicate species such as ferns are extremely sensitive and cannot easily tolerate chemicals.

Your choice of pesticides is typically between two types of materials. Contact pesticides work by coating pests such as mites and whiteflies with poisons. Systemics must be absorbed by the plant and ingested when the foliage is sucked or chewed; use these to combat pests such as scale. Both types of products can be used to treat infestations of pests such as mealybugs.

NONCHEMICAL CONTROLS

Plants grown indoors simply can't stand up to harsh chemical treatments. To prevent unnecessary (sometimes fatal) damage to their delicate tissues, begin with the control method that's the least toxic yet most beneficial to your plant. Here are some alternative ideas.

- Besides hand picking, you can also vacuum up insects to physically remove them from your plants. Use gentle suction and try it out on a small test area first, to be sure your plant can withstand vacuuming before you treat the entire plant.

- For a persistent problem with thrips, set out yellow sticky cards (the color attracts thrips) to snare the tiny insects. You can purchase the cards at garden centers and nurseries.

- Insecticidal soap sprays and horticultural oils work largely by smothering mites and insects. "Botanical" products have the advantage of breaking down quickly in the atmosphere. Two examples are neem—an extract from the seeds of the neem tree (Azadirachta indica)—which interrupts the growth cycle of insects, killing the larval and pupal stages; and pyrethrum—the dried flowers of Chrysanthemum cineraiifolium—which paralyzes insects. Always use products specifically formulated for houseplant use, and treat your plants in a cool location (preferably outdoors) out of direct sun.

- Certain fungal diseases can be treated with nontoxic materials. Sulfur, for example, is effective against powdery mildew; it's included in some commercial soap sprays. More powerful synthetic fungicides are often less harmful to plants than are insecticides, but fungicides pose a greater risk to human health and should not be applied indoors.

Use insecticidal soap in a tub of water to bathe small plants that have insect infestations. Slosh plants upside down through the solution to dislodge and kill the pests, let the plant rest for several minutes, and then rinse with tepid water. Repeat the process until all insects are removed. Soft or bottled water is more effective than hard water.

Pest and Disease Problems

PROBLEM	DESCRIPTION	CONTROLS
Aphids	Tiny, soft-bodied insects may be green, reddish, or black, and round or pear shaped. They cluster on new growth to suck out plant juices; stunted, curled, or distorted leaves result. Sticky honeydew secretions appear as droplets on or beneath the plants, attracting ants.	Hose off with water; or spray with soap, pyrethrum, diazinon, or malathion (in increasing order of toxicity).
Crown or stem rot	Soft, brown discoloration near base of stems, usually caused by constantly wet soil; leaves may yellow and drop. Plants seldom recover, though you may be able to nurse mild cases back to health.	Cut out lightly damaged areas, wash off all old soil, and repot plant in a fast-draining mix; set it a little higher in the new soil. Take cuttings of healthy growth as a backup. Water less in the future.
Cyclamen mites	Relatives of spiders, both adult pests and eggs resemble fine dust on the undersides of leaves, often with webbing; leaves become deformed, brittle, and scabby. Cyclamen, geranium, fuchsia, chrysanthemum, and African violet buds may wither and drop.	Destroy affected leaves. Isolate plant and spray light infestations with a miticide. Severe infestations are extremely difficult to control; destroy the entire plant.
Gray mold	Furry gray covering on leaves, stems, or flowers of fleshy, soft-leafed plants (such as African violet, gloxinia, and begonia) caused by too cool or too humid growing conditions.	Destroy all diseased parts. A fungicide labeled for treating gray mold (botrytis) on houseplants may be used. Warmer temperatures, lower humidity levels, and good ventilation help prevent and control spread of disease.
Mealybugs	Tiny white, cottony insects cluster in leaf axils, beneath leaves, and on stems and roots to suck plant juices. They cause stunted growth and yellowed and withered leaves; their sticky honeydew attracts ants. Unchecked, mealybugs can kill a plant.	Wash plant with soap or water spray; or remove bugs with a cotton swab dipped in denatured alcohol; or spray with a light horticultural oil, diazinon, or malathion (in increasing order of toxicity). Cut away infested roots.
Scale	Covered with yellowish or tan, crusty shells, scale insects appear as bumps on stems and leaves. They suck plant juices and excrete a sticky honeydew that attracts ants and fosters the growth of a black, sooty mold.	Scrape away or wash off scales with soapy water or remove them with a cotton swab dipped in denatured alcohol. Use horticultural oil sprays or a systemic insecticide, according to label directions.
Spider mites	Spider-relative colonies form on undersides of leaves, often with webbing. Unless you use a magnifying glass, they appear to be dustlike specks. Damage shows up as pale and stippled leaf surfaces and sometimes as stunted growth. Dry heat favors infestations.	Isolate infested plants; wash them with a miticidal soap-and-water spray. Raise the humidity level and lower the ambient temperature.
Thrips	Barely visible unless shaken off plant onto a white piece of paper. Thrips' rasping and puncturing distorts leaves and discolors flowers, often causing a puckered appearance.	Wash plants with water or soap sprays. Treat heavy infestations with diazinon or malathion (in increasing order of toxicity); spray twice, at 10-day intervals.
Whiteflies	White flying adults and nonflying young stationed on leaf undersides suck plant juices and excrete a sticky honeydew. Plant's foliage yellows and drops.	Wash plants with water or soap sprays every few days when insects are present; use malathion in severe cases. For continuous protection, keep yellow sticky cards near plants.

FAVORITE
HOUSEPLANTS

As you explore the rich, diverse world of houseplants, you'll find exotic jungle and desert species in addition to familiar old favorites such as ivies and violets. This chapter offers a full description of dozens of fascinating genera— that is, major plant groups— as well as hundreds of popular varieties within those groups. You'll find care instructions that specify the type of light and potting mix, the temperature range and humidity level, and the amounts of fertilizer and water that best suit these plants. Included, too, are pointers on when to repot and how to propagate.

Because common names sometimes differ from region to region—or even from one nursery to the next—plant groups are listed here by their botanical name. If you only know a plant's common name, look it up in the index (pages 111–112), which will direct you to the correct listing in this chapter.

Browse through to narrow down your shopping list before you buy new plants, matching their growing needs with the environment you can offer in your home or workplace. For the basics on caring for any houseplant, review the information on nurturing and maintenance on pages 19–51.

Baskets of blossoms and pots of foliage create a visual feast of houseplants.

AESCHYNANTHUS

(ESS-kuh-NAN-thubs)
LIPSTICK PLANT, PIPE PLANT,
ZEBRA BASKET VINE
Gesneriaceae

☙ If bud drop is a problem,
check for sufficient soil moisture
and humidity. If no flower buds
appear at all, give your plant a few
hours of direct sun each day.

Long, cascading stems bearing shiny, fleshy leaves and dramatic tubular flowers characterize this group of plants from subtropical forests of Southeast Asia. The main blooming season begins in summer, but flowers may appear sporadically throughout the year. Aeschynanthus looks its best in hanging baskets or set atop a pedestal to show off its dangling, unbranched stems (up to 2 feet long) and showy red blossoms. Where light is inadequate, grow compact varieties under fluorescent tubes.

Aeschynanthus

PLANT CARE. Aeschynanthus thrives on the same care you would give its close relatives, the African violets. It requires a lightweight soilless mix (peat-based for acidity) and conditions that mimic those of its native habitat—bright reflected light (but outdoor shade) and high humidity. You'll need to mist frequently or use humidity trays to supply enough atmospheric moisture in dry interior environments. Check the potting mix regularly: it should be constantly moist during the spring and summer growing season and during blossoming, but dry on top in fall and winter. After flowering, prune back leggy stems; cut the oldest one or two back to the base. Propagate by stem cuttings.

During the growing season, apply low (quarter-strength) doses of an acid fertilizer weekly, or opt for proportionately lower doses with each watering. Water more sparingly in late autumn and winter, and, if possible, move plants to a cooler (60°F/16°C) site while they rest. Repot and trim roots in late winter or early spring. Sucking insects—aphids, thrips, mealybugs, and aphids—are attracted to lipstick plant.

SPECIES AND VARIETIES. *Aeschynanthus lobbianus* 'Variegatus' bears clusters of deep red blooms and dark green foliage marbled in creamy white. It's called lipstick plant because of the way its flowers emerge from their calyxes, like lipsticks from their tubes.

AGLAONEMA

(ag-lay-o-NEE-muh)
CHINESE EVERGREEN, PAINTED
DROP TONGUE
Araceae

☙ A saplike exudation from leaf
tips, especially in *Aglaonema
modestum*, will spot wood finishes,
so be careful where you place pots.

Aglaonema commutatum 'Maria'

Attractive foliage and toughness account for aglaonema's perennial popularity. Its graceful, oblong leaves grow from a central stem; depending on the species, the leaves may be solid medium green or splotched with various shades of gray and green. The flowers—mostly insignificant—resemble small, greenish callas with red berries. This somewhat slow-growing plant can eventually reach a height of 2 to 3 feet, but it usually stays lower.

PLANT CARE. Like most houseplants, aglaonema is true to its tropical origins. It prefers average room temperatures, filtered light, and high humidity; yet even in poor conditions, it performs admirably. This is one of the very best choices for difficult, low-light environments. If the cream or gray ornamental splotches fade on your plant, however, move it into brighter light (but out of direct sun; its foliage burns easily).

Pot aglaonema in a fast-draining, soil-based medium in a slightly undersized pot; allow the mixture to dry out partway before rewatering. Except in winter, apply a complete fertilizer regularly. This undemanding plant needs repotting only every 2 or 3 years. You can easily propagate it by placing cuttings in a container of plain water, removing and potting up shoots when they root; or you can air-layer the leafless, cane-like stems. For good health and best appearance, wipe the leaves frequently with a damp cloth. Watch for occasional bouts with aphids, mealybugs, red spider mites, and scale.

SPECIES AND VARIETIES. *Aglaonema commutatum,* the brightest-foliaged and most popular species, has glossy leaves about 8 inches long, splashed with pale green, gray, or yellowish green markings. The variety 'White Rajah' has white markings; 'Treubii' has bluish green leaves with silver splotches.

A. *crispum,* painted drop tongue, has leaves approximately 12 inches long, variegated with gray and green. Attractive 'Silver Queen' has grayish green leaves daubed with silver.

A. *modestum,* the old-fashioned Chinese evergreen, is recognizable by its solid green, waxy leaves. The glossy foliage of this species undulates slightly along the leaf margins.

Aglaonema commutatum 'Silver King'

Looking as exotic as its origins (Mexico and South America), colorful aphelandra is dressed in showy, waxy green leaves with striking, broad white veins that account for its common name. Its crowning touch is a showy spike of long-lasting, red-tinted yellow bracts that surround smaller, short-lived yellow flowers—all on a thick, nearly black stem. These plumelike spikes, which sometimes appear on side shoots as well as terminally, begin their spectacular bloom in late summer, often continuing sporadically throughout the year. In tropical regions plants grow tall, but as houseplants they rarely exceed 1 or 2 feet; many are low enough to fit into terrariums.

APHELANDRA
(AF-uh-LAN-druh)
ZEBRA PLANT
Acanthaceae

PLANT CARE. Evenly moist soil (a high-humus, soil-based medium), high humidity in a warm setting, and bright filtered light (or morning sun) will keep your plant vigorous. To promote flowering, apply a balanced liquid fertilizer every 2 weeks and repot annually after flowering, replacing as much of the old potting mix as you can. When flower bracts eventually fade, cut back their stalk to a pair of sturdy leaves to keep plants bushy. Reduce watering and fertilizing in winter and move your plant to a cooler location—55° to 60°F (13° to 16°C).

Aphelandra squarrosa

Aphelandra must have constant access to moisture during its growth and bloom periods, but it's also sensitive to poor drainage and will rot in a too-moist planting medium. If your soil mix is soggy, add extra perlite or lava rock for faster drainage when you repot.

You'll want to propagate aphelandra every few years, because older plants decline rapidly and lose their appeal. Cuttings from stem tips root easily if taken between late winter and late spring. You'll prevent fatal wilting if you pinch back the foliage on cuttings by one-third to one-half and cover cuttings with clear plastic while you wait for new roots and leaves to form. Under stress, plants can be bothered by spider mites, aphids, scale, and mealybugs.

SPECIES AND VARIETIES. *Aphelandra squarrosa* 'Louisae' is the best-known cultivar, but newer varieties 'Apollo White' and 'Dania' are more compact, with more pronounced white veining. Veins are more silvery on 'Snow Queen' and cover more of the leaf; its flowers are paler yellow.

As its common name implies, cast-iron plant is strong—one of the sturdiest and most carefree of all houseplants—and long-lived, though somewhat slow growing. Its tough leaves— glossy and dark green with distinct parallel veins—reach 1 to 2½ feet long and 3 to 4 inches wide; they're supported by 6- to 8-inch-long grooved and elegantly arching leafstalks. Flowers are insignificant.

ASPIDISTRA
(as-puh-DIS-truh)
CAST-IRON PLANT
Liliaceae

PLANT CARE. Indoors, aspidistras are loved for their cast-iron constitution in difficult situations where most other plants would fail. Despite their preference for bright light (but no direct sun), average daytime and cool nighttime temperatures, high humidity, and moderate water, these tolerant plants also do well in dim light and cool temperatures. On the

Cast-iron plants aren't always classed as houseplants. If you don't see them in the houseplant section at your nursery or garden center, look among the outdoor shade-loving plants. In mild-winter climates, *Aspidistra elatior* is hardy out-of-doors year-round, in full or heavily filtered shade.

other hand, they'll merely survive in high heat, dry air, and dry soil. Regular fertilizing applied in low doses helps them look their best. In winter, keep plants cool and reduce watering, allowing the soil to dry nearly completely.

Don't worry about repotting cast-iron plant. Unless conditions are ideal and your plant thrives beyond expectation, it can live for years in the same pot and soil-based mix. When crowding occurs, divide clumps of rhizomes in spring; wait until they're growing vigorously before fertilizing. Pests and diseases are seldom a problem if you keep fertilizer to a minimum and neither over- nor underwater.

Aspidistra's large, smooth leaves attract dust in a hurry; keep them clean with a soft, damp cloth. (Don't use commercial leaf shine products.) If the pointed tips become dry and brown, you may have overfertilized or overwatered, particularly during autumn and winter. Trim tips with a sharp scissors.

Aspidistra elatior

SPECIES AND VARIETIES. *Aspidistra elatior* 'Green Leaf' is a medium green variety; 'Milky Way' (or 'Minor') bears creamy speckles on dark green foliage. Several variegated cultivars show their pale colors in broad streaks down leaf centers or along margins; they'll lose this variegation, however, if you plant them in a humus-rich, highly fertile soil.

BEGONIA
(buh-GO-nyuh)
Begoniaceae

An angel-wing begonia

Begonia is a huge and diverse group of hundreds of species and thousands of cultivated varieties. Its many members are prized for their textured, multicolored foliage and clusters of exquisite flowers, but relatively few types are widely sold. In the descriptions that follow, you'll find mention of popular begonias along with a few others that are less commonly available.

Such a large genus of plants obviously needs a system of descriptive categories. Botanists divide begonias in one way for study and generic classification; plant societies divide them in another for exhibition purposes. For practicality, they are commonly divided into broad groups according to their root structure: fibrous, rhizomatous, and tuberous.

Fibrous-rooted types include the wax begonias or semperflorens types (widely used as summer bedding plants), the angel-wing begonias with canelike stems, and the shrubby begonias commonly grown in baskets.

Rhizomatous begonias are subdivided according to size as well as the foliage characteristics of various types; they include the so-called star begonias. Another subgroup comprises the popular rex begonias.

Tuberous types vary widely and include numerous hybrid crosses; they're known for their showy, sometimes flamboyant flowers.

Among these broad groups, you'll find miniatures and sprawling trailers, 6-foot or taller canes, climbers and bushy clumps, as well as upright and creeping fleshy and woody stems. Variations in flower type range from small dangling clusters to showy solitary blooms. Leaves in all three groups are generally asymmetrical, one side being noticeably larger and rounder than the other. However, other leaf differences among groups are considerable: leaf pairs that resemble angel wings, stars, and small rounded lobes; leaves delicately textured, richly colored, and intricately patterned; and foliage with spots, hairs, and waxy coatings. Flowers are either male or female, which is significant for most indoor gardeners only because male blossoms are showier and drop early, whereas female flowers generally persist on plants far longer, often for many weeks. The groups discussed here are subgroups of the three broad groups above; they are divided to reflect plant habit and structure.

PLANT CARE

Many types of begonia have become favorite houseplants because they adapt easily and thrive in ordinary indoor conditions; other, more sensitive, ones are collected for their unique foliage. As a group, they're satisfied with average room temperatures during bloom and active growth—65° to 75°F (19° to 24°C)—and bright filtered or reflected light (they also grow well under fluorescent tubes). They like a fast-draining, moist, peat-based potting mix and a dilute but steady supply of nutrients. Neither soggy nor dry soil suits them. When water collects in the saucer beneath the pot after watering, pour it off promptly; probe the soil before rewatering, and do so only when the top of the soil is completely dry. Use shallow pots for planting your begonias, because they tend to have shallow roots; repot in spring.

If begonias make any extra demand, it's for increased humidity. Some miniatures and several specialty types prefer terrarium conditions, and almost all others require humidity trays or misting, especially during warm weather and in dry winter air. In damp climates, however, they're prone to mildew or gray mold if conditions become too moist or if air circulation is insufficient. Consult the specific group descriptions that follow for additional care guidelines.

CANE-TYPE BEGONIAS. These plants owe their name to their stems, which grow tall and woody and develop prominent, bamboolike joints. The group includes begonias once classified as angel-wing types—those with paired leaves resembling extended wings. Erect on multiple stems, these plants sometimes reach 5 feet or more. Most cane types bloom profusely in large clusters of white, pink, orange, or red flowers. The usual bloom season is early spring through autumn, though some types bloom virtually year-round. Encourage compact growth by pinching young tips, and rejuvenate mature plants by pruning old canes to the base after flowering.

REX BEGONIAS. Plants in this group of hybrids are grown for their bold, multicolored leaves, some of the most striking of all begonia foliage. Often called painted-leaf begonias, they have amazing leaf features: contrasting bands and waves of brilliant colors, spiral arrangements, and textured edges. Most, but not all, have rhizomatous roots; crosses with *Begonia* Rex Cultorum Hybrids and related species have yielded hybrids with various tendencies, including winter dormancy.

A rex begonia hybrid

Rex begonias need high humidity and bright light for healthy foliage and rich coloration; they'll languish in dry air. Place pots on humidity trays or mist plants frequently. You may need to experiment somewhat before finding the right light intensity for your plant; some species develop a heightened metallic sheen in low light. (See "Rhizomatous Begonias," below, for basic care.)

RHIZOMATOUS BEGONIAS. These plants grow from a rhizome (an underground stem) and are valued primarily for their beautiful foliage, though many have attractive flowers as well. Members of this group perform well as houseplants and are fairly easy to care for. They need bright light and average room temperatures. Because they have shallow roots, it's best to plant them in wide, shallow pots. Water only when the top inch of soil is dry, and never let pots sit in water or the rhizomes will rot. Flowering forms bloom from winter through summer, the season varying among specific types. Flowers

A cane-stemmed begonia in a hanging basket

TRIMMING FOLIAGE

Browned leaf edges, always unattractive, can show up on your houseplants for several reasons. They usually signal underwatering or a salt buildup in the potting mix, but sometimes this marred foliage is merely a natural response by some tropical plants to being confined in nontropical quarters.

You can improve your plant's appearance by shearing off browned leaf edges with a very sharp scissors, following the natural shape of the leaf. Aglaonema, aspidistra, dracaena, and cordyline are a few of the foliage plants needing periodic trimming.

Semperflorens begonias

appear in clusters on erect stems above the foliage. The rhizomes of many species will grow over the edge of the pot so that the plant eventually becomes bell shaped. If you prefer, you can cut back these creeping stems.

SEMPERFLORENS BEGONIAS. These used to be called (and still are, to some extent) bedding begonias for their outdoor use and wax begonias for their succulent, waxy stems. They produce small flowers from spring through early autumn in shades of red, pink, and white. Numerous hybrids (*Begonia* Semperflorens-Cultorum Hybrids) are bushy, from 6 to 15 inches tall, with green, red, bronze, or variegated foliage.

SHRUBLIKE BEGONIAS. This large group of fibrous-rooted begonias is characterized by multiple stems that are soft and green rather than bamboolike, as in the cane-type group. Popular for both their foliage and flowers, shrublike begonias have interesting leaves: some are heavily textured, others sport white or red hairs, and still others develop a soft, feltlike coating; many come in eye-popping shapes and textures. Though most grow upright and bushy (some as tall as 8 feet), others are less erect and make outstanding hanging-basket plants; pinching helps keep them compact. In early spring, prune the branches back halfway for greater fullness. Flowers appear in white and shades of pink, red, or peach; they can unfold at any time of year, depending on the variety.

WINTER-FLOWERING BEGONIAS. Among the various groups of tuberous begonias, Rieger hybrids (*Begonia* × *hiemalis*) are favored indoors for their winter blooms. Flowers on these hybrids average about 2 inches across and appear over a long season, including winter. When a healthy, mature plant is in bloom, its green leaves and stems are all but invisible under a blanket of blossoms. In the cool winter months, give these bushy, compact plants plenty of direct light, but in summer give them indirect light. Let the top inch of the soil dry out between waterings, but with each watering soak the soil thoroughly; remove any water standing in saucers. (Be careful not to sprinkle the leaves with water; this plant is prone to leaf spot diseases.) If your plant gets rangy, cut its stems back to 4-inch stubs. You may be more satisfied, though, if you discard your old plant and start over with a new one. Many named varieties are available.

A tuberous begonia hybrid

BROMELIADS
(bro-MEE-lee-adz)
Bromeliaceae

The showy pink bracts and lilac blossom of a *Tillandsia*

Bromeliads are members of the *Bromeliaceae* family, a plant group primarily from the tropical Americas. In nature, these colorful plants often exist as lithophytes—plants attached to rocks—or as epiphytes—plants that find their homes on the trunks and branches of trees. Unlike most other plants, bromeliads rely very little on their roots, absorbing water and nutrients directly through their foliage. Many have the unusual habit of collecting moisture in the center of leafy rosettes, where they hold it around their growing tips.

Perhaps the bromeliads' most remarkable feature is their flowers—spikes of small petals with large, showy bracts—which rival their handsomely patterned foliage for interest. Most species bloom only after several years; they may then die back, yielding to smaller plants (called pups) that sprout from the sides of the mother plant.

PLANT CARE

Average indoor conditions suit most bromeliads, which tend to be sturdy and undemanding. Generally, the more leathery and silvery their foliage, the greater their need for bright light; thinner, more tender foliage must be given filtered sun. Growth slows under two conditions: when light is less intense in winter and when sunlight is too severe in summer.

Bromeliads enjoy moderately warm conditions. Locate them where temperatures always stay above 55°F/13°C; those with thin foliage will suffer serious damage in cooler conditions. High humidity is essential for these tropical plants. As warm temperatures increase, you'll need to increase the humidity level and frequency of watering.

In general, water all bromeliads when the top half-inch of the soil feels dry to the touch—except in winter, when they need little moisture and can tolerate drier soil. Use rainwater or bottled distilled water for irrigating and misting; hard water causes unsightly spots on the leaves. Keep the central, cuplike receptacles of species such as *Neoregelia* and *Nidularium* filled with moisture. Feed most bromeliads year-round with half-strength doses of a liquid fertilizer (see the care instructions for specific types below). Pour the fertilizer solution on the planting medium and splash or spray it over the foliage and into the central leaf cups as well.

You can grow nearly all bromeliads in a peat-based mixture in pots, though some, such as tillandsias, do well and are more striking when fastened to a tree branch or bark and mounted or hung for a distinctive display. Pests are rarely a problem, but watch for scale and mealybugs.

SPECIES AND VARIETIES

Of the dozens of plant groups in the bromeliad family, the following ones are most commonly available in nurseries and garden centers. Specialty growers have longer lists of additional species and varieties in their catalogs.

AECHMEA (eek-MEE-uh). Epiphytic in nature, aechmeas have rigid, strap-shaped leaves (often with spiny margins) that form a funnel of foliage around a central tube, which—in the tropics—catches rainfall. Indoors, plants like to have this vase filled with moisture. At bloom time, a plumelike flower (mostly showy bracts) rises from the center and provides a colorful accent for several months. Gracefully arching leaves on many species reach 12 to 18 inches; they vary in color from deep green to pale gray. Keep aechmeas in bright sunlight, or they won't flower. Withhold fertilizer for 1 to 2 months during winter.

Aechmea chantinii has gray green foliage with bands of white underneath; its flowers are bright orange to yellow, with showy red bracts.

A. fasciata, called urn or vase plant, has silvery scales that fall off to leave green bands on the lilac gray leaves; white, woolly stems hold dense clusters of bluish purple or red flowers with rosy pink bracts.

BILLBERGIA (bil-BUR-gee-uh). These spectacular bromeliads vary considerably from species to species. Unusual in nearly every way, they're among the most resilient of all houseplants, able to survive despite neglect; when well tended, they reward you with kaleidoscopic color in both foliage and flowers.

Old-time favorite *Billbergia nutans,* known as queen's tears or Cleopatra's earrings, has narrow leaves with silvery bronze overtones; rose, green, yellow, and violet flowers spill out of rosy red bracts. Hybrid billbergias also offer spectacular color: 'Fantasia' has urn-shaped, coppery green foliage blotched with cream and pink; its violet blue flowers emerge from red bracts. Tubelike 'Muriel Waterman' has stiff, upright, plum-colored leaves banded in silver; small blue flowers appear atop pink bracts.

CRYPTANTHUS (krip-TAN-thus). These stemless, terrestrial bromeliads are called earth stars for the shape of their flattened, leafy rosettes. Offsets appear within the leaf axils or emerge from creeping underground rhizomes. Cryptanthuses require less water than do most other bromeliads, and very little if any fertilizer. Plant them in shallow pots; repot in wider containers or divide plants as colonies form.

TOP: *Aechmea fasciata* 'Morgana'
BOTTOM: A *Billbergia* hybrid

RAIN FOREST CONDITIONS

Unless you have a greenhouse in which you can control temperature and moisture with ease at any time of year, your bromeliads may yearn for extra warmth and humidity. You may never be able to give them rain forest conditions, but try setting these plants out-of-doors during a gentle summer rain. If your tap water has neither excessive salts from softening nor excessive alkalinity from minerals in hard water, give bromeliads a light shower or fine spray at the kitchen sink. Misting with tepid distilled water at any time will also clean their foliage and promote vigor.

TOP: *Cryptanthus zonatus*
BOTTOM: *Cryptanthus bivittatus*

A FULL CUP

Bromeliads with cuplike or vase-shaped central tubes like to have a constant supply of water surrounding their growing tips during active growth. (This type of standing moisture would rot most other plants.) For the healthiest of conditions, refresh this stored water from time to time by turning your plant upside down, pouring out the old supply, and refilling the cup or tube. Distilled water or rainwater is best.

ABOVE: *Nidularium innocentii*
RIGHT: *Guzmania* 'Cherry'

The foliage on species such as *Cryptanthus acaulis* is a muted green or gray or bears a reddish tinge; others *(C. bivittatus* and *C. bromelioides tricolor)* are striped in green and gray, sometimes flushed with pink. *C. zonatus* has dark brownish red, wavy-edged leaves banded crosswise with green, brown, or white; its cultivar 'Zebrinus' has more pronounced striping. Cultivars of other species also offer exceptional foliage colors, but the flowers of all types are insignificant.

DYCKIA (dye-KEE-uh). Looking very much like spiky succulents, the dyckias bear little resemblance to other members of the bromeliad family. They do grow in open rosettes, but their stiff leaves—short and triangular or long and lance shaped—are lined with sharp teeth along the margins. Their foliage is covered with a gray, scaly "scurf," which gives them a silvery cast. Most species available as houseplants spread in low, stemless rosettes. Stalked, yellow to orange, bell-shaped flowers appear in spring. Native to dry tropical regions, these plants like bright light (direct sun is best), low humidity, and little water year-round; withhold fertilizer during winter. Add extra grit to their potting mixture to ensure speedy drainage.

Dyckia fosteriana

GUZMANIA (guz-MAY-nee-uh). Long, narrow, flexible leaves characterize the popular guzmanias from the Andean rain forest. The foliage on some forms is solid green; on others, it's striped in pale green or red. White or yellow flowers surrounded by brightly colored red, orange, or yellow bracts are borne on stalks—either tall or short—in summer.

Guzmania lingulata is the most popular species and one of the most variable. Its foliage may be bright green or striped in reddish violet; the leaves arch out 18 to 24 inches, somewhat wider than the plants are tall. Star-shaped flowers with many rows of bracts along the stems make a colorful show. Naturally occurring varieties and hybrid cultivars offer additional flower and foliage combinations.

NEOREGELIA (nee-oe-ruh-GEE-lee-uh). Neoregelias are grown for the striking color contrasts of their foliage. In some species, such as *Neoregelia carolinae, N. concentrica,* and *N. princeps,* brilliant rosy red or purplish tones cover the cuplike centers and the base of each leaf radiating out from dense, funnel-shaped rosettes. In others, such as *N. spectabilis* or fingernail plant, the leaf tips are red. The foliage of many species bears colorful stripes and flecks as well as spines and teeth along the margins. Named cultivars may be more compact and may bear decorative banding and brighter or darker color tones. The flowers (usually insignificant) appear within the cuplike center, which should always be filled to the top with water.

NIDULARIUM (NID-yu-LAIR-ee-um). Plants in the *Nidularium* group are similar to the neoregelias but have more prominent leaf sheaths that form a deeper funnel-shaped receptacle in the rosette centers. At flowering time the leaf bases turn bright red, and small, leafy, bright red bracts that look very much like petals surround smaller, insignificant blossoms. After several months, the flowering rosettes die back, leaving behind young pups.

TILLANDSIA (til-LAND-zee-uh). The most common houseplants among the hundreds of diverse tillandsias are the air plants—small-growing species that form tight, leafy rosettes. These have few if any roots and thin, often highly colored and thread-like foliage.

Tillandsia

Tillandsia ionantha is a dwarf plant with 2-inch leaves that become suffused with pinkish red before flowering; their violet blue blossoms appear above rosy red bracts.

T. multicaulis has medium green leaves 12 to 16 inches long, which arch around funnel-shaped rosettes. Exquisite floral spikes of tubular blue flowers are dominated by overlapping red floral bracts.

Vriesea splendens

VRIESEA (VREE-zee-uh). One of the most outstanding plant groups among the bromeliads, the dazzling vrieseas make excellent houseplants. Showy foliage and bright, exceptionally long-lasting blossoms create an exotic tropical effect. Easy to care for, vrieseas need several hours of sunlight daily and ample water during the warm growing months; they also like to have the funnel-shaped vase within their stiff, arching foliage filled with moisture. During the winter rest period, water just enough to keep the potting mixture from drying out completely.

Two *Neoregelia* species illustrate the foliage variation in this plant group.

The best-known members of the *Cactaceae* family are desert plants that grow as spiny globes and columns, sometimes branching and very often assuming curious and picturesque shapes. They share their niche in the houseplant world, however, with their less formidable-looking cousins, the more smooth-stemmed jungle cacti. The latter hail from a radically different environment, though both types are native to North and South America.

The main appeal of jungle cacti (one of them, the Christmas cactus, is a household favorite) lies in the exuberant color of their ravishingly beautiful, tiered blossoms—whereas most of the desert species are grown less for their cup- or bell-shaped flowers than for their incomparable stem shapes and textures. Some cacti blossoms are cherished for their scent; many are night blooming. Specialty growers offer long lists of species and cultivars of all types; if you can't find what you seek, it helps to know that several groups are labeled and sold under more than one name.

Cacti are specialized succulents—plants whose structural adaptations allow them to store water and withstand periods of drought. None has true leaves; instead, stems assume the photosynthetic role that leaves normally play. These stems become thick and fleshy, a modification that, though important in their native habitats, is insignificant in the home or office environment. Yet it is these adaptive growth characteristics that endear them to the home gardener.

The cacti differ from other succulent plants in one significant way: they develop specialized surface areas called areoles, slight depressions on the stems that give rise to flowers and tufts of bristles or spines. These are most notable in desert cacti, because they're arranged in either vertically aligned rows or patterns of warty outgrowths called tubercles. The spineless types develop hairy protrusions. On jungle cacti, the areoles are difficult to see, tucked away along the sides of the stems.

CACTI
(KAK-tye)
Cactaceae

Mammillaria elongata
'Pink Nymph'

Mixed cacti

PAIN-FREE POTTING

Cactus spines and bristles can be an awkward nuisance as well as a painful one when it comes time to take cuttings or remove plants from their containers. Exercise a few precautions to protect your fingers while you work with these prickly plants.

∾ Wear protective gloves—or at least one heavy glove. (You may want to keep one hand free to manipulate a small hand tool.)

∾ Use tongs to loosen offsets. Many cacti quickly form these young plantlets around their base: you can root and then plant them to increase your collection.

∾ To lift a cactus, fold a newspaper into a long, narrow strip and wrap it around the prickly stems. Grip the ends of the paper close to the cactus, as you would grasp a long handle.

DESERT CACTI

Dozens of plant groups in the *Cactaceae* family have evolved various but similar mechanisms to help them survive in adverse, arid conditions. Their most noticeable features are the prickly surfaces and shapes of their distinctive stems. Some assume a low, globose mound in youth, later maturing as columns in colonies; others tend to spread out as offsets, or plantlets, appear around their base. Still others branch with age, but many never change their shape. The flowers on some types commonly appear indoors, yet on others rarely form. Though most cacti are valued as landscape plants in dry climates, a more limited number find their way to indoor gardens.

PLANT CARE. Reserve the sunniest site you have for your potted cactus garden; these desert plants thrive and bloom only with ample sunshine. Unable to tolerate low indoor light levels, they are nonetheless satisfied with low indoor humidity and average room temperatures. Though it's true that desert cacti can endure long dry spells, it's equally true that they must have liberal supplies of water during spring and summer for annual growth and bloom. They cannot, however, stand constant wetness; be sure to let the soil dry out almost completely between waterings. During late autumn and winter, give cacti a rest period in a cool location (below 50°F/10°C) and water only enough to prevent the soil from remaining completely dry; watering early in the day allows surface moisture to evaporate. Except in winter, apply half-strength doses of fertilizer monthly.

Cacti need a fast-draining planting medium, the key to preventing rot. A standard mix consists of 1 part coarse sand or perlite, 1 part garden loam, and 1 part leaf mold; add 1 tablespoon of ground limestone and 1 tablespoon of bonemeal to each gallon of the mixture. You may want to spread a layer of grit or fine gravel over the soil surface to speed drainage. Remove cacti from their containers every year or two to examine their roots; repot them in fresh mix if the roots are compacted. You can detach offsets from the parent plants in spring and root them in a standard potting medium. After removing the offsets (some must be cut off; others detach easily with tongs), allow their cut stems to rest for a few days to develop a callus before rooting and potting. Always use the smallest possible container so that the roots are not subjected to excessive moisture. Besides rot diseases, scale and mealybugs sometimes bother cacti.

APOROCACTUS (uh-POR-oe-KAK-tuhs). This abundantly blooming, long-stemmed plant group from Mexico has been tagged rat-tail cactus for its cylindrical, sometimes stringy, pendent stems; nonetheless, it is one of the most beautiful cacti when in bloom. The tubular blossoms have tiers of purplish pink or red petals. It's best to plant young aporocacti in small pots, nurture them patiently, and transfer several at a time to a hanging basket after they've become established. In a few years, their cascading stems will be 2 to 3 feet long, decked out beautifully with short spines at areoles all along their length. Set the plants in filtered sun for most of the year, but move them to lower light while they rest in winter. (Their stems will turn yellow in too much sun.) Repot every year or two in a humus-rich but fast-draining potting soil. Cuttings root easily.

Aporocactus flagelliformis

ASTROPHYTUM (AS-troe-FYE-tuhm). Looking very much like its common names, bishop's hat or star cactus, these cacti form small, unbranched hemispheres with four to ten ribs on bulging side segments. Potted astrophytums stay fairly small and bloom on and off throughout the summer. They like moderate water and light feeding during the warm months; give them full or filtered sun.

Astrophytum asterias, also called sea urchin or sand dollar cactus, has six to ten spineless ribs that spiral from top to bottom and are lined with white, buttonlike areoles. The stems are dotted with pale scales; the flowers are yellow with orange or red throats.

A. myriostigma is the easiest species in this group to grow and the one most resembling a bishop's hat. The five swollen stem segments (the number can vary from three to ten) are covered with minute, chalky, scalelike hairs that give it a grayish color. The ribs of mature specimens are spineless, the flowers bright yellow.

Astrophytum myriostigma

CEPHALOCEREUS (SEF-uh-loe-SEER-ee-uhs). Called old man cactus, this is one of the most popular cacti among beginning collectors. Grayish white, hairlike growths cascade down the sides of *Cephalocereus senilis,* bestowing a shaggy-dog look on this columnar cactus. The hairy "beard" conceals closely set, bristly spines along numerous vertical ribs. Cephalocereus grows slowly, seldom exceeding 12 inches indoors, and can stay in the same size pot for several years. Add extra lava rock, fine gravel, or perlite to the potting mix for fast drainage; moderate water and fertilizer during the warm months will speed growth. Flowers will not appear on these plants indoors.

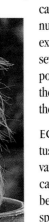

Cephalocereus senilis

ECHINOCACTUS (EK-uh-noe-KAK-tuhs). Called barrel cactus, this group contains some of the most satisfying cacti to cultivate for classic spine-filled, symmetrical forms. Only the juvenile cacti of four species are suitable as houseplants, however, because in maturity they are too large for indoor culture. A fifth species *(Echinocactus grusonii)* can be grown indoors for many years. These cacti need a cool winter rest—between 40° and 50°F (5° and 10°C)—to maintain their spherical shape. Always allow the soil surface to dry thoroughly to prevent rot at the base of the stem. Spines develop their brightest color in full sun.

Echinocactus grusonii is a slightly flattened species known as golden barrel cactus. It's covered with golden yellow spines that emerge from areoles on knoblike tubercles. As these slow-growing plants age, the tubercles appear in vertical rows along 20 or more ribs. Golden spines at the top cluster like a tufted crown; flowers rarely appear.

E. horizonthalonius is the only species likely to bloom indoors. Deep pink, bell-shaped flowers appear in summer. The stems are grayish green and lined with 7 to 13 broad ribs and brown spines. This species grows 6 to 10 inches tall and up to 16 inches wide.

ECHINOCEREUS (EK-uh-noe-SEER-ee-uhs). Members of this large, popular group of "hedgehog" cacti form free-branching clusters or mounds of either upright or prostrate stems, rarely taller than 1 foot. All species are covered with dense, highly ornamental spines. Their compact appearance and easy care make them a favorite potted plant. Large, showy, tubular flowers to 4 inches wide appear on short stems; flowering is heaviest in full sun on plants that are watered liberally in spring and summer. Add ample fine gravel (not sand) to the planting mix for excellent drainage. Numerous species and varieties exist.

ECHINOPSIS (EK-uh-NOP-suhs). Called both sea urchin and Easter lily cactus, this large group has species heavily spined on prominent ribs; they bloom in dramatic, often large and highly colored funnel-shaped blossoms. (Considerable confusion surrounds the names of many of these species, which previously were included in other cactus groups, including *Chamaecereus, Lobivia,* and *Trichocereus.*) All types need similar care. Give them maximum exposure to sunlight for heaviest flowering, strong stems, and rigid spines. Though they thrive in hot weather, these cacti must have a cold winter rest for sev-

TOP: *Echinocactus grusonii*
BOTTOM: *Echinocereus engelmannii*

Echinopsis chamaecereus

Mammillaria haageana

Melocactus matanzanus

A *Mammillaria* with seedpods

eral months at temperatures above freezing but below 50°F/10°C if they are to flower. Give a resting echinopsis very little water, if any; during the warm months, water moderately when the soil dries slightly. Apply light doses of a balanced fertilizer every 2 weeks.

Echinopsis chamaecereus (or *Chamaecereus silvestrii*) is a clustering, columnar type called peanut cactus for the shape of its young offsets. Short, light green joints branch from the base to produce fingerlike clumps 6 to 12 inches high. This species is ribbed and spiny, spreads quickly, and blooms in flamboyant scarlet; plant it in a gritty soil mix in a very shallow pot or dish for fast drainage. Cuttings can be taken and rooted immediately, without waiting for cut surfaces to callus over.

GYMNOCALYCIUM (JIM-noe-kuh-LIS-ee-uhm). Plants in this group are usually called chin cacti for the chinlike bulges below each spine cluster. They're grown for their plump ribs, spectacular spines, and enchanting flat or bell-shaped flowers. Most are small, squat plants that bloom at an early age, making them ideal houseplants.

Gymnocalycium saglionis is one of the largest cacti in this group; its chubby, solitary stems reach 1 foot in diameter. Outstanding features are the reddish brown, thickened, hooked spines (reddish yellow on young plants) and knobby chins atop flat-topped stems crowned with a ring of blush-toned blossoms.

MAMMILLARIA (MAM-uh-LAIR-ee-uh). This plant group—one of the largest and most interesting in the cactus family—has long been favored for indoor culture, partly because most of its members are less than 1 foot tall. Individuals may be solitary or clustered; spines may be soft bristles or thorny hooks; flowers are arrayed like crowns consisting of a few single flowers or a full circle of delicate blooms. Many types branch at the base or produce colonies in clumps.

Gymnocalycium

Lacking the ribs characteristic of many types of cacti, mammillarias instead bear spines on warty outgrowths (tubercles) that spiral around the stem. Flowers emerge from separate sets of areoles on the previous year's growth. Despite their great diversity of form, all mammillarias have the same cultural needs: a coarse, sandy soil mix, infrequent but adequate amounts of water, sun year-round, and a cool rest in winter.

Mammillaria bocasana is an old favorite known as powder puff or snowball cactus. Its bluish green stems are covered with white, radiating spines and bristly hairs.

M. elongata (gold lace cactus) forms clumps of variable-shaped stems, most often cylindrical and elongated with pale yellow to reddish brown spines.

M. haageana is slightly taller than wide and often solitary, though clusters may form.

M. hahniana is a stout, white-haired, solitary globe called old lady cactus. Short spines cover the medium green stem under its hairy coating. Purplish red flowers bloom in the warm months, adding a distinctive color accent. This elegant species forms young offsets in maturity.

MELOCACTUS (MELL-oe-KAK-tuhs). Dubbed melon cactus, individuals in this plant group are solitary and spherical, with prominent, spiny ribs. Flowers form on a woolly, caplike structure (called a cephalium) atop the stem, which elongates to more than a foot in some species. This stem growth stops once the cephalium appears; glossy berries follow the flowers. Among the 30 species you'll find colorful features such as bluish gray stems; spines in red, brown, and yellow; and an orange, brown, or white cephalium studded with contrasting bristles.

OPUNTIA (oe-PUN-tee-uh). Widely grown as a landscape plant, opuntia also basks contentedly in a sunny window as a houseplant. Simply make sure that it soaks up sufficient light to keep its branches firm; they become spindly and misshapen in low light. These cacti are generally characterized by flattened, padlike shapes, though some are more spherical or cylindrical. Spines and flowers appear over the surface of the flattened segments, very seldom on the ribs; flowers rarely form indoors. Handle these cacti with extreme care: their barbed bristles (called glochids) are difficult to remove if they puncture your skin.

Opuntia basilaris, beaver tail cactus, has nearly spineless segments; gray or purplish pads with reddish glochids appear where the spines would normally grow.

O. microdasys, bunny ears or prickly pear cactus, branches profusely to form a dense living sculpture. Numerous 2- to 6-inch flattened, rounded joints are studded with spineless pads covered with tufts of golden or reddish brown glochids.

O. quimilo grows to tree size, but in youth its flattened stem segments make a striking silhouette as a houseplant.

Opuntia quimilo

PARODIA (puh-ROE-dee-uh). Numerous houseplant favorites belong to this expanded group (many formerly classified as *Notocactus*) of low-growing, globose to cylindrical cacti. Some of the finest are covered with hairy or spiny protrusions of silvery white and gold from closely set areoles along the vertical ribs. Most species flower heavily in summer if given ample water and sunlight. Parodias are highly recommended for beginning indoor gardeners.

Parodia concinna (formerly *Notocactus apricus* and *N. concinnus*) is a 3-inch-wide, slightly flattened sphere that produces curved, reddish spines surrounded by a colorful contrasting ring of yellow spines. Yellow flowers blossom on stout 3-inch tubes near the slightly sunken area at the apex.

P. haselbergii (or *Notocactus haselbergii*), called scarlet ball cactus, blooms a bright orangey red. Soft white spines cover this solitary globe-shaped, grayish green species, which is lined with row after row of small, warty tubercles and woolly, white areoles. These cacti develop a slight depression on the crown, which may become distorted with age.

P. magnifica glistens under a haze of pale yellow spines. The bluish green stems grow in clusters and produce yellow flowers.

Opuntia microdasys

Parodia magnifica

JUNGLE CACTI

As houseplants, the cacti of tropical forests play a different role than do their desert relatives. Their thinner stems, though succulent enough to carry them through brief dry periods, are flattened on the jungle cacti, and in most species branch far more freely—thus they are displayed differently, commonly in hanging baskets. The abundant flowers on dangling stems supply the most noteworthy aspect of these unique plants: flamboyance during bloom. Specialty growers offer hundreds of cultivars with blossoms ranging from neon-bright hues to pale pastels and from tiny ones to saucer-size wonders.

PLANT CARE. Unlike desert cacti, the jungle cacti must have protection from strong sun. They do need bright light, however, and they can tolerate brief periods of morning sun; too little light results in spindly growth and poor flowering. Give them average indoor temperatures and high humidity year-round. Except in winter, apply light doses of a balanced fertilizer; substitute a high-potassium fertilizer as the buds form. Water liberally except in winter and after flowering, when plants are at rest and the soil should

An *Epiphyllum* orchid cactus

WATER WAYS

Jungle cacti get their moisture directly from rainwater, and that's how your houseplants would like to get theirs. If you have hard or softened water, your cacti may suffer. Rainwater is ideal, but distilled water can also be used. Here are a few tips to remember when you water your cacti.

∿ Always allow your plants to dry out slightly between waterings; the soil surface should dry completely. Too much water is worse than too little.

∿ While cacti are at rest in winter water them very little, if at all, to forestall growth spurts as well as to prevent stem and root rot.

∿ If you have a tendency to overwater, keep your cacti in unglazed clay pots. Clay allows the soil and roots to breathe, whereas glazing and plastic hold in moisture.

dry out somewhat between waterings. Generally, these cacti need repotting only when their roots fill the container; use a fast-draining soil mix similar to that for desert cacti. Cactus fanciers like to substitute peat or coarsely ground bark for soil and to increase the amount of leaf mold. Propagate these plants by rooting stem cuttings; allow the cut edges to air-dry for a day or two before rooting them. Watch for scale insects.

EPIPHYLLUM (EP-uh-FIL-uhm). Day-blooming hybrids called orchid cacti make up most of the houseplants in this unique group of plants. (Night-blooming types are also available.) They are grown for their radiant, iridescent, cup-shaped blossoms, many having multiple layers of petals and throats of contrasting colors; some look like radiating stars. The stems are long, flattened, often triangular, and notched along the edges; they reach 2 feet or more in length and must be staked for upright growth. These cacti adapt easily to a range of conditions, though they need cool nights in winter for bud formation and spring bloom. Before the buds begin to form, in very late winter, give these plants one or two doses of a nitrogen-free fertilizer (such as a 0-10-10 formula).

Growers like to group orchid cacti by flower size and color. Extra-small and small blossoms appear on compact plants, which are useful where space is limited; these tend to bloom early. Medium to extra-large blossoms appear on larger plants. Epiphyllums bloom in all colors except shades of blue. Those colors and cultivar names are too extensive to be listed here, but mail-order cactus catalogs offer long lists and related supplies.

A *Hatiora* hybrid

HATIORA (HOT-ee-OH-ruh). Also known by its earlier name, *Rhipsalidopsis*, this small plant group is referred to as Easter cacti, though it is often included in a larger group called holiday cacti. Hatioras' cultural needs are typical of all jungle cacti, with one important exception: these plants must have filtered light only—no direct sun. Most hatioras are hybrid cultivars that put on spectacular spring displays of bell-shaped flowers—some almost daisylike—that appear for weeks and nearly cover the plant. The flowers open during the day and close at night. The succulent stems are nearly flat, sometimes winged, and always segmented, with hairy brown bristles at each end; the blossoms are produced at the tips of new growth. Numerous hybrid cultivars are valued for their variations in flower shape and color—mostly in red tones but also in pinks, lavenders, and purples.

SCHLUMBERGERA (shlum-BUR-juh-ruh). Beloved as year-round houseplants, the schlumbergeras—called Thanksgiving and Christmas cacti—are also prized as flowering holiday decor. These plants, still often sold as *Zygocactus*, remain attractive when not in bloom; their flat-jointed, branched stems arch gracefully. Growth habits vary from strong and upright to wide spreading and drooping; the stem color may be bright green or take on a purplish cast. Their easy culture and high success rate has made schlumbergeras popular with beginning gardeners.

For the best performance, withhold fertilizer from early fall until after the bloom period, and provide nighttime temperatures between 55° and 60°F (13° and 16°C). When the plants come into bloom, you can move them (gradually) to a warmer location. The short-tubed flowers with spreading, pointed petals bloom from November through March. Besides white, blossoms come in many shades of pink, salmon, yellow, orange, red, and purple.

Schlumbergera × *buckleyi* and its cultivars are the Christmas cacti. These plants have slightly rounded and scalloped stem segments. *S. truncata* and its cultivars are called Thanksgiving or crab claw cacti for their 1- to 2-inch-long, sharply notched stem segments; the tip segment features two large "teeth."

A *Schlumbergera* hybrid

Native to tropical America, this large group of short-stemmed plants is known for striking foliage. Individual leaves show intricate markings in shades of green, white, pink, purple, and maroon. The undersides of some types are solid purplish red, contrasting with the patterned surfaces. New leaves unfold above older ones, giving the foliage a layered look. Most forms grow upright, with leaves varying in length from 8 to 18 inches. The *Calathea* genus is closely related to *Maranta* (see page 85) and is often confused with it. Both genera are grown for their foliage; the flowers are insignificant.

PLANT CARE. Calathea performs well in either a soil- or a peat-based potting mix and in warm, even temperatures of 70° to 75°F (21° to 24°C). Filtered or reflected light encourages the richest leaf color; too-abundant or too-intense light will damage leaves. Most importantly, calathea requires high humidity and protection from drafts. Mist it frequently and place the pot on a humidity tray.

Keep potting soil constantly moist but not soggy. Except in winter, apply a liquid fertilizer diluted to half strength every 2 weeks. If leaf margins turn brown, compare your plant care practices with those described here. Repot as necessary in late spring to avoid a pot-bound condition. If plants are too crowded, divide clumps. Watch for signs of mites, mealybugs, and aphids; treat before the foliage is damaged.

SPECIES AND VARIETIES. *Calathea makoyana*, commonly known as peacock plant, has 10- to 12-inch oval leaves. Foliage colors include pale olive green, cream, and purple displayed in featherlike, blotchy patterns with a broad, darker green border along the margins.

C. majestica (or *C. ornata*) stands out among foliage plants. Its erect, glossy leaves, which reach nearly 2 feet in length, are beautifully marked in varying shades of green.

C. zebrina, familiarly called zebra plant, is compact in habit, with elliptical leaves 1 to 2 feet long and half as wide on a 1- to 3-foot plant. Upper leaf surfaces are velvety green with pale yellowish green and olive green bars extending outward from the midrib; the undersides are purplish red.

CALATHEA
(kal-uh-THEE-uh)
PEACOCK PLANT, ZEBRA PLANT
Marantaceae

 This is one plant that loves water on its leaves. Spray often, but be forewarned: you may want to use bottled water if your water supply contains fluoride or is high in lime. These minerals can affect calathea's sensitive foliage.

Calathea majestica

A native of tropical North and South America, *Callisia* is related to—and often confused with—*Tradescantia* (page 109). Its stems stand erect when young, drooping as they elongate; mature stems can reach 2 to 3 feet in length. Pointed oval leaves, appearing about an inch apart on the stems, have a striking coloration: their tops are olive green striped with creamy yellow, their undersides purplish. Because of its dangling growth, callisia is best displayed in a hanging basket or on a pedestal. The small flowers are rarely seen.

PLANT CARE. Callisia grows best in filtered light with average humidity and temperatures from 60° to 70°F (16° to 21°C) and about 10°F/6°C lower in winter. It likes lots of moisture, so water plentifully—enough to keep the soil moist at all times—for most of the year. Taper off in winter, when the soil should dry nearly completely before you rewater. Very low doses of fertilizer given once or twice monthly (less frequently in soil-based mixes) will keep your plants growing vigorously enough to warrant pinching stem tips frequently for compactness. These plants seem to quickly grow themselves out of shape and need replacing every few years. If you take stem cuttings at least once a year, you'll have fresh, mature replacements to bring out when older plants look bedraggled. Keep the foliage clean to deter spider mites.

SPECIES AND VARIETIES. *Callisia elegans* is the most commonly grown type. This plant never becomes very tall, as its stems cannot support themselves and trail freely.

CALLISIA
(kal-lis-EE-uh)
INCH PLANT, STRIPED INCH PLANT
Commelinaceae

Callisia

CHLOROPHYTUM

(klor-oe-FYE-tum)
AIRPLANE PLANT, RIBBON PLANT,
SPIDER IVY, SPIDER PLANT
Liliaceae

❧ If you grow chlorophytum in a hanging basket, rotate the basket a half-turn every week or so to produce even, well-spaced growth.

Chlorophytum

Chlorophytum, native to tropical climes around the globe, probably owes its popularity to its unique and fascinating growth habit. The mother plant, a clump of curving leaves that look like long, broad grass blades, sends out curved stems up to 2 feet long with colonies of plantlets at their ends and at nodes along their lengths. Tiny white flowers appear before the miniature plants sprout. To best protect these offspring, grow chlorophytum as a hanging plant.

PLANT CARE. Chlorophytum prefers bright reflected light (morning sun only in winter), standard potting soil, and average house temperatures. Though it will tolerate the low humidity of most homes, it does benefit from frequent mistings. Let the soil dry out a bit between waterings. Apply a complete fertilizer regularly.

Small plantlets at the ends of stems often grow complete with roots that you can snip off and plant at any time; rootless plantlets can be layered (see pages 44 and 46). If you leave the arching stems and "babies" attached, mother plants become full and fountainlike. Repot when swollen tuberous roots lift the root ball and protrude out the drain hole, making it difficult to water. If plants dry out and leaf tips die back, trim off the unsightly ends. Excess salts and fluoride also cause tips to burn. Scale insects occasionally present a problem.

SPECIES AND VARIETIES. *Chlorophytum comosum* 'Mandaianum' is a compact form with much shorter (4- to 6-inch) leaves of dark green with a yellow stripe down the center. 'Picturatum' has longer (12-inch) striped leaves. 'Variegatum' has leaves edged in creamy white; 'Vittatum', the most common form of spider plant, has 6- to 12-inch leaves—green with a broad center stripe of creamy yellow.

CISSUS

(SIS-suhs)
GRAPE IVY, KANGAROO VINE,
OAKLEAF IVY, TREEBINE
Vitaceae

❧ Cissus cultivars are commonly grown as mounding cascades and hanging plants, but you can train them to climb a moss-covered post. At repotting time, set the post in the planting mix in a pot slightly larger than that previously used. Most cultivars can stay in the same pot for years but benefit from annual top dressing (see page 38).

Cissus—related to Virginia creeper, Boston ivy, and grape—comprises a group of evergreen vines popular for their elegant looks and easy care. Most send out tendrils that latch onto any type of nearby support.

PLANT CARE. An easy-to-grow plant, cissus adapts readily to a broad range of indoor conditions. It prefers bright reflected light, average temperatures and humidity, and regular fertilizing. A standard indoor potting soil suits all of the species. Allow the soil to dry out a little before watering: excessive water promotes stem rot, which causes foliage to turn brown and die. Cut back even further on watering and fertilizing during the winter rest period.

Cissus rhombifolia

Keep up with fast-growing stems by snipping off growing tips to force side branching and fullness. Some of the more vigorous types may develop floppy, bare stems—cut these back halfway, just above a swollen stem node and a vigorous leaf. Give plants an occasional shower to keep their leaves clean and lessen the chance of spider mite infestation.

SPECIES AND VARIETIES. *Cissus antarctica*, sometimes called treebine or kangaroo vine for its bounding growth, is native to Australia and is the most popular species. Its medium green leaves resemble those of a grapevine, and its tendrils will climb if they have something to grab onto. Pinch off growing tips to foster bushier plants. 'Minima', a dwarf form, has waxy green leaves and a compact growth habit.

C. rhombifolia, commonly known as grape ivy, puts forth dark green leaves with toothed edges in groups of three. Reddish hairs grow from the undersides, giving the foliage a bronze cast. This species grows rapidly, even in low light. 'Ellen Danica' produces compact, bushy growth with darker green leaves that are less lustrous but more deeply lobed (resembling oak leaves).

One of the most glamorous and exotic houseplants, clerodendrum is a native of West Africa. If left untrimmed, this large evergreen vine will grow to 10 feet or more. It has attractive dark green, heart-shaped leaves, but its brilliant flowers are the primary attraction. Scarlet 1-inch tubes, surrounded by white calyxes, are borne in flattish 5-inch-wide clusters, usually from August through October.

PLANT CARE. Grow clerodendrum where you can give it bright filtered light, warm temperatures, and some humidity spring through summer. Keep the soil-based potting medium thoroughly moist but not soggy. Except in late autumn and winter, apply a complete fertilizer regularly. During these cool seasons, give your plants a rest in a very cool spot: 50° to 55°F (10° to 13°C). Let the soil dry almost completely between waterings. As soon as new growth appears (usually in early spring), move the plant gradually from its resting place (increase a few hours each day) to a warmer and brighter spot. If you place your plant outside for the summer, watch for whiteflies, mealybugs, aphids, and spider mites.

If you're growing clerodendrum for its lovely flowers, put a little extra effort into providing good humidity and pruning it. During spring and summer, keep a humidity tray under the pot or mist frequently. There are several ways to shape this plant: you can train it to a trellis, let it spill from a hanging basket, or encourage a compact, shrubby shape by frequently pinching off its growing tips. Because clerodendrum grows rapidly and vigorously, it can become rangy. It looks best with attentive pruning, pinching, and grooming. After flowering, cut the vines back halfway; completely remove one or two of the oldest stems every year in spring, when you repot.

SPECIES AND VARIETIES. Of the hundreds of species, only *Clerodendrum thomsoniae* is well suited for houseplant culture.

CLERODENDRUM
(kler-o-DEND-ruhm)
BLEEDING HEART VINE,
CLERODENDRON, GLORYBOWER
Verbenaceae

> ❧ You may find that you have more blossoms if you keep mature bleeding heart vines in a 6- or 8-inch pot and in a slightly pot-bound state.

Clerodendrum thomsoniae

This South African native of the amaryllis family draws attention year-round to its dramatic dark green, strap-shaped leaves that can reach as long as 18 inches. In bloom, clivia becomes one of the most spectacular houseplants. Clusters of yellow to brilliant orangey red, funnel-shaped flowers open atop stout stalks that rise from the center of dense foliage clumps. These sensational blossoms appear from December to April, peaking in March or April.

PLANT CARE. Clivia thrives in a rich, fast-draining, soil-based potting mix. For the loveliest blooms and healthiest foliage, set pots in bright, reflected light; morning or late-afternoon sun is ideal. (Move plants out of direct sun if you notice leaf scorch.) Provide average humidity and a warm room: 70° to 75°F (21° to 24°C). During the active growing season in spring and summer, apply a complete fertilizer regularly and keep the soil moist but not soggy.

In late autumn, clivia begins its essential cool-season rest period, which continues into winter. During this time, give it slightly different care. Move containers to a location where light is less intense and the temperature is a fairly constant 50°F/10°C for approximately 1½ to 2 months. Also let the soil mix dry out almost completely before watering just enough to moisten.

In early spring, gradually move your plants to a brighter, warmer area; wait until the flower stalk is about 6 inches tall before watering and fertilizing normally. After flowering, clip off

Clivia miniata

CLIVIA
(KLYE-vee-uh)
KAFFIR LILY
Amaryllidaceae

> ❧ Clivia is one plant that grows best when its clumps are left undisturbed in the same pot for years. Crowded roots seem to promote flowering, whereas dividing and repotting often delays blooming for several years. When you do repot (no oftener than every 3 to 5 years), handle the brittle roots gently to minimize breakage.

A *Clivia miniata* hybrid

any berries that form, but leave the flower stalk intact until it dies back completely. If you have the space, you may want to move pots of clivia out-of-doors after the last frost in late spring, situating them in protected spots on covered patios and decks. After a few days of acclimation, you can set them among ferns and rhododendrons in shaded beds and borders.

Generally pest free, clivia occasionally hosts red spider mites, mealybugs, or scale. This plant is slightly toxic, causing stomach upset if ingested and dermatitis if its sap contacts skin.

SPECIES AND VARIETIES. *Clivia miniata* is the most commonly available species; the variety 'Aurea' produces lovely yellow blooms in various shades. It may take a little searching to find other species that bloom in coral, red, and yellow.

CODIAEUM
(koe-dee-EE-uhm)
CROTON, GOLD DUST PLANT,
JOSEPH'S COAT
Euphorbiaceae

✺ Whenever possible, move your croton out-of-doors into lightly filtered shade for the warm seasons. Bright light intensifies the foliage color and invigorates plants; deficient light weakens them, causing the lower leaves to drop.

One of the most wildly colorful small shrubs in the houseplant world, codiaeum offers abundant variety of shape, pattern, and hue. Its large leathery and glossy foliage on 2- to 3-foot bushy stalks are a study in flamboyance! No two leaves are ever the same. You will find them in limitless combinations of green, yellow, red, purple, bronze, and pink with contrasting veins, variegation, and mottling. Leaves on some plants are long and narrow; on others, they're oval or lance shaped, their edges straight, wavy, twisted, or notched into three deep lobes. Flowers are insignificant.

*Codiaeum variegatum
pictum*

PLANT CARE. To grow codiaeum indoors, it's a good idea to mimic tropical conditions as closely as you can: give plants bright light (2 to 3 hours of direct sun daily), warm temperatures (never below 55°F/13°C), high humidity, and plentiful water so that the soil always stays moist but pots never sit in water. Mist your plants frequently to raise humidity, and wipe their leaves with a damp cloth to discourage pests. Aphids, leaf miners, mealybugs, red spider mites, and thrips may occasionally bother plants, especially those under stress.

Plant codiaeum in a standard planting mix and fertilize regularly, except in winter. (Allow plants to rest in winter by withholding fertilizer and reducing watering.) Mature plants can remain in 8-inch pots indefinitely, though they benefit from an annual top dressing. Propagate from cuttings or by air layering.

SPECIES AND VARIETIES. *Codiaeum variegatum pictum* varies from plant to plant, but named cultivars have their own characteristic coloration, leaf markings, and shapes.

COFFEA
(KAW-fee-uh)
COFFEE PLANT, COFFEE TREE
Rubiaceae

✺ Pinching the tips regularly during active growth in spring and summer restricts height and promotes fullness.

Famous for its beans, coffea is a relative newcomer to the houseplant scene. This native of East Africa willingly adapts to indoor life, and its glossy foliage makes an exceptionally handsome display. The coffee plant can be raised from unroasted coffee beans, because it is in fact the same "tree" that produces coffee for commerce. Though single stemmed, coffee tree is naturally bushy and shrublike. Under cultivation it can reach 15 feet, but indoors it rarely surpasses 4 to 6 feet.

The coffee tree bears dark green, glossy foliage similar to that of its close relative, the gardenia. The distinctly ribbed leaves grow to about 4 inches long and 2 inches wide. Given optimal conditions, your plant will maintain its highly polished look for years, eventually flowering and bearing fruit.

PLANT CARE. Like gardenia, coffea prefers bright filtered sunlight, a soil-based potting mix rich in organic matter, plenty of humidity, and an even temperature (normal room temperature is perfect). Unlike gardenia, however, it requires constant, even moisture (except in winter, when the soil should nearly dry out between waterings). Apply a complete fertilizer regularly, but during spring and summer only.

Coffea is a pleasing, trouble-free plant when conditions are right, but it's particularly sensitive to fluctuations in temperature and air quality. It will drop leaves if temperatures fall below 55°F/13°C for extended periods or if the surrounding air is too dry or drafty. Set pots on humidity trays and mist plants frequently to keep the foliage richly green and lustrous.

SPECIES AND VARIETIES. *Coffea arabica* 'Nana', a smaller version of the coffee tree, is sometimes available. Flowers and fruit appear on this dwarf before it reaches 2 feet in height.

ABOVE AND LEFT: *Coffea arabica*

Closely resembling *Aeschynanthus* (see page 54), the large group of flowering columneas from the American tropics are excellent candidates for hanging baskets and other trailing displays. Sparsely foliaged stems on various species either arch horizontally or dangle beneath their containers in an elegant, weeping fashion.

Plants in this group produce leaves in various shapes, with glossy or hairy surfaces. The hooded, tubular flowers—in shades of red, orange, yellow, or combinations of these—appear in abundance, looking somewhat like tiny goldfish, and are the main attraction. The primary bloom period is autumn, but the most popular varieties produce flowers nonstop throughout the year.

PLANT CARE. Columnea prefers bright reflected light—up to 14 hours a day—and just a bit of direct sun in winter for best flowering. These plants thrive in average room temperatures, but they must have high humidity to look their best. Use humidity trays or mist daily with tepid water. (If you notice any leaf spots, discontinue misting and supplement air moisture with a humidifier, if necessary.) Water containers only moderately, allowing up to one-third of the soil to dry out; use liquid fertilizer in half- or quarter-strength doses at watering time unless your plant has finished bloom and is resting.

You'll need a well-aerated soil mix for this often epiphytic (one that grows on other plants) tropical plant. Light peat- or bark-based mixes with perlite and vermiculite or compost allow the best root growth. Replace the mix annually when you repot or root-prune. Check periodically for aphids, leaf miners, mealybugs, and cyclamen mites.

SPECIES AND VARIETIES. *Columnea* 'Aladdin's Lamp', one of the most breathtaking cultivars, produces the largest and showiest red flowers among the hybrids. It blooms year-round.

COLUMNEA
(kahl-UHM-nee-uh)
GOLDFISH PLANT, NORSE FIRE PLANT
Gesneriaceae

If you plan to grow columnea under fluorescent lights and need to economize on space, choose a compact variety. The dwarf 'Mary Ann' is scarlet red and semitrailing; compact and upright *C. linearis* 'Purple Rose' bears rose pink flowers.

Columnea 'Early Bird'

CORDYLINE

(KOR-duh-lyen)

GOOD LUCK PLANT, HAWAIIAN TI, TI PLANT, TREE-OF-KINGS

Agavaceae

❧ Species with solid green foliage tolerate direct sun easily, but varieties with colored foliage will burn; give the latter indirect or filtered light.

Cordyline terminalis 'Kiwi'

Looking almost like palms with narrow, sword-shaped leaves and canelike, sparsely branched trunks, these relatives of agave and yucca make dramatic, supersize houseplants. Their ultimate height varies depending on the species. Some are often confused with their close relatives, the dracaenas, and are even called dracaena. Cordyline rarely blooms indoors.

Cordyline terminalis

PLANT CARE. Though it will tolerate low-light conditions, cordyline prefers at least 4 hours of bright, filtered sunlight per day. Despite looking like a desert plant, it is not drought tolerant; in fact, cordyline depends on a constant supply of humidity in the surrounding air and a moist soil mix—except in winter, when the soil should dry out somewhat between waterings. Fertilize lightly, during active growth only.

If you want cordylines to stay smaller and more manageable, keep plants in undersized pots that will restrict their roots; to encourage normal growth, repot annually using a soil-based potting mix. When a plant becomes too large to repot, refresh its soil with an annual top dressing. You can increase the numbers of your plants by rooting 2-inch sections of stem cuttings taken from pruned canes. Check plants periodically for scale, spider mites, and other sucking insects. You may notice leaf discoloration if your water contains fluoride.

SPECIES AND VARIETIES. *Cordyline australis* has a graceful, fountainlike habit in youth; in maturity, the upper leaves rise stiffly whereas the lower foliage arches and drapes. This species needs space for its 3- to 6-foot-wide foliage tufts and tall stems. Its potentially massive size can be contained if you cut its stems back to force multiple trunks to grow. 'Atropurpurea', called bronze dracaena, has bronzy red foliage; 'Baueri' is a deep purplish red. Plants in this species can take full sun.

C. terminalis, commonly known as the ti plant, is usually started from "logs"—small sections of mature branches—imported from Hawaii (see "Taking Leaf and Stem Cuttings," page 45).

CROSSANDRA

(kross-SAN-druh)

FIRECRACKER FLOWER

Acanthaceae

❧ Firecracker flower grows so fast that you can plant seed and enjoy blooms in less than a year. If you sow seeds, keep the growing medium moist and warm—75° to 80°F (24° to 27°C). Don't give up if sprouts are slow to appear; germination takes from 20 to 60 days.

A native of India, this evergreen plant is a relatively new arrival on the houseplant scene. Its overnight popularity is hardly surprising, considering its gardenialike glossy, deep green, slightly wavy-margined leaves and long bloom potential. In spring, coral to scarlet orange flowers with bright yellow eyes pop out of four-sided stalks in clusters of two or three; each flower may reach 2 inches or more across. Floral spikes produce blooms for about 2 weeks, but under the most favorable conditions flowering continues throughout the year.

PLANT CARE. To keep crossandra really healthy, give it a few hours of direct sun daily in winter and bright indirect light the rest of the year. Moist, but not wet, soil and a humid environment with average room temperatures (never below 65°F/19°C) will encourage a long bloom period. Naturally shrubby, crossandra needs no pinching, but plants will be shorter and fuller if you do pinch tips on very young plants. Indoors, its height rarely exceeds 18 inches.

If you start fast-growing firecracker flower in a 4- or 5-inch pot in a soil-based mix, you'll never need to repot it; just top-dress annually. Apply half-strength doses of liquid fertilizer

Crossandra

every 2 weeks during bloom and active growth; withhold fertilizer during the winter rest period and water just enough to keep the soil from drying out completely. Besides starting crossandra from seed, you can root stem cuttings in spring or early summer. In hot weather, look for red spider mites; scale, whiteflies, and mealybugs are infrequent pests.

SPECIES AND VARIETIES. *Crossandra infundibuliformis* is the only commonly available species for growing indoors. 'Mona Walhead' is more compact than the species and bears deep salmony pink flowers.

CTENANTHE
(tuh-NAN-thuh)
BAMBURANTA, NEVER-NEVER PLANT
Marantaceae

Grown mostly for its unusual leathery foliage, ctenanthe is a close relative of the more extravagantly tinted maranta and calathea. Plants in the *Ctenanthe* genus can be recognized by their narrower leaves with herringbone patterns in shades of green; some varieties have yellow markings and reddish undersides. The plants may start as several short stalks, each producing a long stem, or as one tall, upright stalk with thin, branching stems; the maximum size is 3 feet high by 2 feet wide.

> ❧ Like other members of the *Marantaceae* plant family, ctenanthe abhors strong light. Not only is its foliage livelier and more radiant in filtered light, but intense light will cause its leaf edges to crisp and curl.

PLANT CARE. Ctenanthe likes bright filtered light, average house temperatures of 65° to 70°F (19° to 21°C), a standard indoor potting soil, and high humidity. Increase the humidity by misting frequently or by placing the pot on a humidity tray. Keep the potting soil moist but not soggy and never too dry. In winter, allow the soil to dry out almost completely between waterings. Except in winter, apply a complete fertilizer regularly in half-strength doses. Pests rarely bother ctenanthe, but it is sensitive to unstable cultural conditions such as drafts, drought, and overfertilization.

You can begin new plants in two ways: by separating basal offsets or by rooting stem cuttings. Choose offsets with a well-formed root mass, cut or break them off from the parent plant, and pot them separately in a soil-based medium. Cuttings should be taken from flowerless stems with three or four leaves.

Ctenanthe oppenheimiana 'Tricolor'

SPECIES AND VARIETIES. *Ctenanthe burle-marxii*, from Brazil, eventually reaches about 2 feet. Its leaves are grayish green, feathered with dark green, sickle-shaped markings; the leaf undersides and leaf stems are maroon to deep purple.

C. oppenheimiana is a more robust and branching plant, with colorful silver bands on dark green foliage. Its cultivar 'Tricolor', the never-never plant, has a more arresting appeal than other ctenanthes. Its leaves show patches of cream and pale green on darker leaf surfaces whose undersides are burgundy red.

DIEFFENBACHIA
(deef-uhn-BAK-ee-uh)
DUMB CANE, DUMB PLANT, TUFTROOT
Araceae

Fascinating foliage, generous size, and good tolerance of indoor conditions has kept dieffenbachia in steady favor as a houseplant. Its leafy green foliage is among the most striking of all indoor plants'. Colors fall within the appealing range of dark green to chartreuse, with intricate variegations in creamy white and yellow. Most dieffenbachias produce single, canelike stems that become slightly woody as they age and drop their lower leaves. Vertical growth is largely unpredictable—some plants grow slowly and may not exceed 2 feet, whereas others race to the ceiling. Flowers that look like narrow calla lilies appear on mature plants.

PLANT CARE. Though dieffenbachia foliage suggests delicacy, these plants can endure considerable abuse and will hold onto life despite poor environmental conditions. Superb-looking plants must have bright light but protection from direct midday sun, which will burn leaves. In winter, however, morning and afternoon sun may be necessary, especially in northern climes. Turn their pots occasionally for even growth all around.

Unlike most other houseplants, dieffenbachia rarely rests, but grows unceasingly. Regular fertilizing in half-strength doses and consistent watering—when the potting soil feels dry to the touch—along with warm temperatures of 65° to 80°F (19° to 27°C) and high humidity keep plants in best form. Provide some extra humidity by misting frequently, and keep the foliage clean. Avoid overwatering, which causes slow growth, undersized new foliage, and legginess.

You can improve the looks of leggy plants by concealing bare stems with lower-growing, bushier plants—or you can reduce the size of the plants themselves by propagating them in any of several ways: Cut the canes back to 6 inches above the soil line, and new stems—usually multiple—will sprout. Other methods are to take stem cuttings from the tips, with a few leaves attached at the top; to root sections of canes having at least one growth bud; and to air-layer stems just under the upper tuft of leaves. Pot new plants in a fast-draining potting mix, and repot them when roots begin pushing the plant above the soil. Dieffenbachia is usually pest free, but watch for mealybugs.

SPECIES AND VARIETIES. *Dieffenbachia amoena,* the tallest species (to 6 feet), bears colossal 18-inch leaves with narrow white stripes slanting toward the center.

D. maculata and its many cultivars fill the houseplant shelves in nurseries and garden centers. Leaves of this species are generally 10 inches long, with greenish white flecks and patches. 'Exotica' is a compact form with dull green edges, a creamy white midrib, and greenish white variegation. 'Rudolph Roehrs', yellow-leafed dieffenbachia, is pale chartreuse blotched with ivory and edged with green.

Dieffenbachia 'Starbright'

Dieffenbachia 'Tropic Snow'

DRACAENA
(druh-SEE-nuh)

BELGIAN EVERGREEN, CORN PLANT, DRAGON TREE, GOLD DUST DRACAENA

Agavaceae

Palmlike dracaena comprises a varied group of decorative-foliage plants, some forming a graceful fountain of broad, curved, ribbony leaves occasionally striped with chartreuse or white. Others have very stiff, sword-shaped leaves and are shrubby or treelike; their stems are often bent, a few looking very much like leafy stalks of corn. Their easygoing nature and interesting silhouettes account for their wide appeal. Large specimens look particularly dramatic in high-ceilinged, contemporary interiors; smaller types are effective in arrangements with other compatible plants, adding subtle contrast in texture and shape. Flowers almost never appear on these houseplants.

PLANT CARE. Dracaena prefers bright indirect or filtered light; in dimmer light there is some loss of vigor. Its other requirements are typical: average room temperatures, high humidity, moist potting soil, and regular low doses of fertilizer (except in winter).

Make a point of keeping dracaena's smooth leaves dust free by cleaning them regularly with a damp cloth or giving them a tepid shower. (It's best not to use commercial leaf shine products on this—or any—plant.) If your dracaena's leaves develop brown tips from underwatering or overfertilizing, simply trim off the brown areas with a pair of scissors, following the natural shape of the leaf. Overwatering will cause the leaves to yellow and drop; continuous soggy conditions cause the roots to rot.

Leave small dracaena species in small (5- to 6-inch) pots, but repot larger species into progressively larger containers until a convenient maximum size is reached. Use a soil-based mix for repotting and top dressing. Propagate from

Dracaena deremensis 'Warneckii'

stem cuttings. Pests are not a significant problem, but foliage may show some discoloration from an excess of fluoride and boron and/or a deficiency of calcium.

SPECIES AND VARIETIES. *Dracaena deremensis* offers several named varieties. 'Warneckii' and 'Bausei' are the most common and are very similar 4-footers; the former has two white stripes on 2-foot leaves, the latter only one.

D. cincta (or *D. marginata*) is one of the easiest dracaenas to grow and consequently is suitable for offices and public buildings as well as homes. It has a slender, gray, canelike stem that often bends as it grows, sometimes reaching 10 feet or more and achieving a striking architectural effect. Its stems terminate in crowns of narrow, leathery leaves ½ inch wide and up to 2 feet long. These thin leaves are glossy green edged in purplish red. 'Tricolor' (or 'Candy Cane') adds pink and cream stripes to shades of green.

Dracaena reflexa 'Song of India'

D. fragrans has an upright blond trunk from which sprout heavy, ribbonlike, bluish green leaves 2 inches wide and 18 to 36 inches long. It tolerates darker indoor situations than do other kinds of dracaena. 'Massangeana', the popular corn plant, is recognizable by a broad, yellowish green stripe down the center of each leaf. Other cultivars show bright variegation.

D. reflexa makes a majestic houseplant until it outgrows its space. (Its ultimate height is 25 feet.) The shiny foliage curves gently inward; the leaves on 'Song of India' are edged in white.

D. sanderiana, Belgian evergreen, has comely, strap-shaped leaves of glossy green striped in silvery white. Its graceful nature makes it resemble a delicate young corn plant, though the cultivar 'Borinquensis' has a stiffer habit.

Dracaena 'Tricolor'

These easy-to-grow evergreen vines are similar in appearance and climbing habit to their relative, *Philodendron;* but epipremnum leaves are shinier, and the common species are beautifully colored with gold and cream tones. On juvenile plants, the leathery, heart-shaped leaves stay small, about 4 to 6 inches long, but on mature plants they become enormous—up to 30 inches long—and deeply lobed. In the tropics these vines climb tall trees, grasping the bark with their fleshy aerial roots. Indoors, you can train them into wreaths and up poles, or let them dangle from hanging baskets. Don't expect showy flowers; these houseplants don't bloom.

PLANT CARE. One of the best-natured and most easygoing houseplants, epipremnum requires no special care and withstands considerable neglect. To keep its foliage lush and glistening, set it in a location with bright filtered light and average room temperature and humidity. The leaf colors fade when the light is either too dim or too intense. Allow the top of the soil to dry out between waterings—except in winter, when plants want to rest and must have nearly dry soil. Fertilize lightly during active growth, but reduce the dosage if leaf tips burn.

Keep the leaves clean by regularly wiping them with a damp cloth, but don't use commercial leaf shine products. Pinch off growing tips to prevent leggy growth, and cut back unwieldy, bare stems halfway or nearly to the base. Repot young plants once a year in fresh, humus-rich soil after their winter rest period. Pests rarely bother epipremnum.

SPECIES AND VARIETIES. *Epipremnum aureum,* the most commonly available form, has splashes of yellow on bright green, waxy leaves. The foliage of 'Marble Queen' is more creamy white than green and has some yellow and moss green variegation. The leaves of 'Exoticum' are lance shaped, thinner, and a duller green with silver flecks.

EPIPREMNUM
(ep-uh-PREM-nuhm)
DEVIL'S IVY, HUNTER'S ROBE, PHILODENDRON, POTHOS
Araceae

If you root epipremnum cuttings every year or two, you'll always have a young, vigorous plant to replace lanky, older ones. As vines age, the stems and leaf petioles elongate, causing the plants to lose their attractive compact form.

Epipremnum aureum 'Marble Queen'

TOP: An asparagus fern makes a graceful hanging plant.
BOTTOM: *Asparagus densiflorus* 'Meyersii'

ASPARAGUS (as-SPAR-uh-gus). These members of the lily family are commonly called ferns because of their bright green, lacy foliage. Favorites for hanging baskets, they have fleshy roots that allow them to go for short periods without water; they grow better, however, with ample moisture. Trim out old stems to improve their appearance and make room for new growth.

Asparagus asparagoides, smilax asparagus, is known through the cultivar 'Myrtifolius', or baby smilax—the decorative, ferny sprays that florists use. This climbing plant is a many-branched vine with thornless stems to 5 feet or more. It's a good idea to train this species on a trellis; left on its own, it can become a tangled mass. Baby smilax is less vigorous.

A. densiflorus 'Myersii', commonly sold as Myers asparagus or foxtail fern, is known for its clumps of stiffly upright stems to 2 feet. Densely covered with deep green, needlelike leaves, the stems have an elegant, plumelike appearance. Plants in the Sprengeri group of this species, known as Sprenger asparagus or asparagus fern, have arching or drooping stems 3 to 6 feet long; they're favored for their effects in hanging baskets. In bright light, these plants flower and produce red berries; in low light, their needles yellow and drop.

A. setaceus, fern asparagus or emerald feather, is another branching vine that requires support; mature plants climb by spiny stems to 5 feet. Its tiny, threadlike leaves form feathery, dark green, flattened sprays that resemble fern fronds; florists use them as filler in bouquets. 'Nanus' is a compact form and the most suitable one for indoor container culture.

ASPLENIUM (as-PLEE-nee-uhm). Members of this large and variable group of ferns resemble one another only in small details and their need for liberal watering. Called spleenworts, they flourish in terrarium culture but also do well enough outside of them when placed over humidity trays. Unlike many other ferns, these species need a rest period from late autumn to early spring. During that time, reduce watering and withhold fertilizer.

Asplenium bulbiferum, mother fern or hen-and-chicks fern, is a graceful plant with finely cut fronds on black stalks that can reach 2 feet long and 8 to 10 inches wide. This fern is easy to propagate from the tiny plantlets that form on short stems atop the finely divided foliage.

A. nidus, bird's nest fern, is a tender species whose broad, apple green, undivided fronds grow in an open rosette somewhat resembling a nest. The gleaming fronds are quick to show damage, so need careful handling; clean them only after they mature and become stiff. The edges tend to pucker when watering is erratic and roots go dry; likewise, the tips and edges may brown from underwatering or low humidity. Direct sun will bleach the fronds, but low light causes sparse growth.

Asplenium

DAVALLIA (da-VAHL-ee-uh). These ferns put out unusual pale brown or gray, furry rhizomes that crawl along the top of the soil and over the rims of pots and baskets; they look very much like a clasping rabbit's foot, which accounts for their common name.

Davallia trichomanoides, hare's foot or squirrel's foot

Davallia trichomanoides

fern, has intricately cut, filigreed foliage. The stems branch freely and interweave with one another, producing a mass of dancing fronds to 2 feet long and 6 inches wide. To show off the forked, creeping rhizomes, grow this fern in a moss-lined wire basket or hollowed-out log.

NEPHROLEPIS (neff-roe-LEPP-is). These ferns are some of the toughest and easiest to grow; they adapt readily to indoor conditions. *Nephrolepis exaltata,* commonly called sword fern, is a large plant with fronds to 5 feet by 6 inches wide. Its variety 'Bostoniensis',

TOP: *Nephrolepis exaltata* 'Fluffy Ruffles'
BOTTOM: *Pellaea rotundifolia*

or Boston fern, is the classic parlor fern of the 1890s. Its fronds are first erect and then arching in long, graceful cascades. The numerous named forms include several smaller versions, such as the dense and stiffly upright 'Fluffy Ruffles' and the 6- to 8-inch-tall 'Mini-Ruffle'; both offer more finely cut, feathery leaflets.

PELLAEA (pell-LAY-ee-uh). Collectively, these ferns are known as cliff-brake. They usually do not rest in winter. Two, quite different in appearance, are popular as houseplants.

Pellaea rotundifolia, commonly called roundleaf or button fern, is one of the most charming of all ferns. Its fronds feature a wiry, reddish black midrib lined with evenly spaced, rounded, bronzy green leaflets. These fronds measure 1 foot long and about 1 inch across, and may grow upright or horizontally. This species makes a good contrast with other small, fine-textured ferns and broadleaf plants.

P. viridis, green cliff-brake, is more upright, bushier and more typically fernlike; its triangular-shaped fronds are up to 2 feet long. Individual leaflets are grassy green and oval or lance shaped; the fronds' green midribs become glossy black with age. Several cultivars are available.

Nephrolepis exaltata 'Bostoniensis'

PLATYCERIUM (plat-ee-SEAR-ee-uhm). The staghorn ferns are native to tropical rain forests. In that environment, they are epiphytic plants, fastening themselves to the sides of trees and sustaining themselves on leaf mold, other forest debris, and moisture that gathers inside their fronds. Try growing staghorn ferns on a slab of bark, in a hanging basket, or—lacking such alternatives—in shallow pots.

Platycerium has two kinds of fronds on the same plant. One is sterile and merely attaches the plant to its support and collects fallen debris; it is green and flattened in youth, brown and papery with age. An old frond is regularly replaced by a fresh young one. The second type of frond, which appears in multiples and accounts for the common name, is shaped like a stag's horns: forked, lobed, or straplike. These fronds are fertile and are grayish blue to dark green in color.

Staghorn ferns make interesting accents anywhere, including outside on patios or lanais. They are, however, highly sensitive to overwatering and will die if they stay too moist. In spring and summer, moisten the growing medium thoroughly and allow it to dry almost completely before rewatering. In autumn and winter, water only enough to lightly moisten it.

POLYSTICHUM (pol-ISS-tik-uhm). Where conditions permit, these ferns grow prolifically outside as well as indoors.

Polystichum tussimense, the most common houseplant fern in this group, is called dwarf holly fern or Korean rock fern. Its foot-long, triangular or lance-shaped fronds are 6 to 9 inches wide and bear many sharply pointed, divided leaflets in featherlike fashion. This species continues to grow year-round, but it may slow down slightly during winter in northern climates.

PTERIS (TAIR-iss). Sometimes called brake or table ferns, the plants in this group of subtropical or tropical ferns are best suited to dish gardens or small pots.

Pteris cretica, Cretan brake, is a low-growing fern whose 8- to 12-inch fronds bear as many as four pairs of leaflets and one terminal leaflet—each up to 4 inches long, ³⁄₄ inch wide, and tapering to a point. The leaflets of 'Albolineata' are wider and marked with a broad, pale stripe along the midrib.

Platycerium bifurcatum

Pteris

FICUS

(FYE-kus)

FIG, RUBBER PLANT

Moraceae

Cutting back tall stems on *Ficus elastica* helps control its size but also stimulates the flow of a milky white sap. Sprinkling powdered charcoal over the cut surface slows and stops the bleeding.

Unrivaled as indoor trees, the figs reign alone in the breadth of their appeal. Their popularity stems from their deep green, leathery foliage, which holds up well in the low humidity typical of residential interiors. Best known for its reliably tough trees, the *Ficus* plant group also includes equally attractive climbers, suitable as small-scale plants for table tops and hanging gardens.

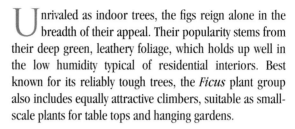

Ficus pumila 'Variegata'

PLANT CARE. Figs are generally easy to grow as long as you tend to their moderate needs. As a rule, most like bright, reflected light and average room temperatures. In low light, variegated forms lose the richness of their contrasting colors. When indoor air is drier than normal in winter or summer, mist the foliage or add humidity trays. Use a standard indoor potting soil. Always test the soil before watering—the top half should be dry (except for *Ficus pumila*—see below). Never allow the soil to become soggy; overwatering causes leaf drop. In winter let it dry out to a greater degree between waterings. Except in fall and winter, apply a complete fertilizer. Watch for scale and red spider mites.

A variegated *Ficus benjamina*

SPECIES AND VARIETIES. *Ficus benjamina,* the popular weeping fig tree, has shiny green, pointed leaves and multiple trunks that spread into an open, many-branched crown. Without pruning, it will reach ceiling height. Weeping fig is one of the most sought-after household plants, despite its troublesome tendency to drop its leaves with the slightest change in temperature, light, or soil moisture. If yours is growing happily, don't move it. If you purchase one, you can expect it to lose foliage from the shock of being moved to your home. Even with no changes, it may drop some leaves once or twice during the year. Give this tree time—several weeks—to recover, and don't proffer extra water out of sympathy. Besides overwatering, avoid drafts, locations near a stove or heat register, or any sudden change. 'Reginald', golden weeping fig, has variegated leaves of creamy lime splashed with dark green.

A variegated *Ficus elastica*

F. elastica, known as the rubber plant, is one of the more foolproof of all indoor plants. It tolerates less light than most plants and less water than most figs. Its dark green leaves are thick and leathery, 8 to 12 inches long by 4 to 6 inches wide, with prominent, depressed midribs. New leaves unfurl from rosy pink sheaths that soon wither and drop. Under optimal conditions, these plants will exceed 8 feet. Named cultivars offer variegated foliage.

F. lyrata, the handsome fiddleleaf fig, performs dramatically indoors with its enormous violin-shaped foliage. Individual leaves may become 15 inches long by 10 inches wide. Prominent veins, puckered surfaces, and undulating margins add to the effect. Cut back the leading stems to induce branching.

F. maclellandii is similar in size and habit to *F. benjamina,* but with longer, wider, and droopier foliage. Unlike most weeping figs, however, the cultivar 'Alii' doesn't drop its leaves when moved; it also takes low light if you let it dry out between waterings. The foliage of 'Amstel King' is wider and more leathery.

F. pumila is a climber: called creeping fig, this many-branched, tiny plant has the capacity to cover a post or a masonry wall in a garden room using its clasping roots. It likes more shade and cooler temperatures than do other fig species; it also needs more water—enough to maintain a thoroughly moist root zone to support its papery foliage. A peat or bark-based soil mix helps it retain moisture.

Ficus lyrata

A popular choice for terrariums, this native of the South American tropics loves humid air. You can grow it successfully as an ordinary houseplant, however, if you mist frequently. The rounded foliage is so compelling that it merits the extra attention it needs to flourish indoors. Its stems are semiupright to trailing. Intricate leaf veining in silvery white and ruby red give fittonia its common names.

PLANT CARE. Fittonia prefers indirect or heavily filtered light; bright light and direct sun can damage the foliage, though plants tolerate brighter light in winter than in other seasons. Keep room temperatures as even as possible for fittonias—about 70°F/21°C (never lower than 55°F/13°C). Outside of a terrarium, supplemental moisture—ideally both a humidity tray and frequent misting—is always necessary to maintain vigor.

Use a standard indoor potting soil that is both well drained and water retentive. Fittonia likes moist soil, but will rot in soggy conditions. When the soil dries excessively, the leaves also dry—then curl and turn brown. Pot plants in small, shallow containers to match their relatively limited root system, and fertilize in half-strength doses every 2 to 4 weeks. Pests are rarely a problem.

SPECIES AND VARIETIES. *Fittonia gigantea*, which grows to 18 inches, is the larger of the two species in this plant group. Its dark green leaves are veined in carmine red.

F. verschaffeltii stays under 8 inches. It has olive green leaves veined in ruby to scarlet. *F. v. argyroneura*, the variety most commonly seen, has bright green leaves with a beautiful silvery white vein network.

FITTONIA
(fih-TOE-nee-uh)
MOSAIC PLANT, NERVE PLANT
Acanthaceae

Fittonias grow rapidly and tend to lose their good looks within a year or two. If you root their stem tips annually, you'll always have a supply of new plants to replace older ones.

Fittonia verschaffeltii argyroneura

An East Indian native, *Gynura* fairly glistens with a mauve opalescence. Its plush, vivid foliage adds an exotic touch to the world of houseplants in its own pot or when combined with greener foliage in a dish garden.

PLANT CARE. For dazzling color and compact growth, expose gynura to a few hours of direct sun each day. Plants become spindly and revert to more green than purple in dim light. They like average room temperatures, high humidity (but no misting—water droplets will mar the foliage), and low doses of fertilizer about every 4 to 6 weeks. Use a standard indoor potting mix and allow the top inch or two to dry out between waterings.

Snip off tips every week or two to prevent legginess and promote side branching. The stems of old plants eventually become woody, but don't let your gynuras live long enough to have that experience; young plants are far better-looking than old ones. Cuttings root so easily and grow so quickly that you can have a new plant in a matter of weeks.

SPECIES AND VARIETIES. The leaves of *Gynura aurantiaca* can grow to 8 inches long, though they're usually smaller. They may be elliptical or heart shaped, but all are coarsely toothed along the margins and densely covered with violet hairs. Left unpruned, the stems will vine and twine on supports to 6 feet or more, or they'll dangle in a hanging basket.

Gynura

GYNURA
(jy-NOO-ruh)
PURPLE PASSION VINE, PURPLE VELVET PLANT
Asteraceae

Besides being unappealing to the eye, the orange blossoms on this purple-toned plant also offend many people's noses with their unusual odor. Try out one or two if you're adventuresome, or nip off the flower buds.

HEDERA
(HED-uh-ruh)
IVY
Araliaceae

🌿 You may be tempted to pot up your ground cover *Hedera canariensis* (Algerian ivy) or *H. colchica* (Persian ivy) and move it indoors as a houseplant. Be prepared for rampant growth if you experiment with either; they'll most likely overwhelm whatever space you give them.

A variegated *Hedera helix*

F ast-growing ivies have made pleasing ornamental plants for many generations. Though it's possible to grow other species indoors, *Hedera helix* (English ivy) is the most common and amenable. Dozens of named varieties exist, offering an ample choice of leaf shape and color. Ivies gracefully climb up poles and trellises or drape over baskets and pots; plant them alone or as a ground cover under indoor potted trees. Almost all types produce aerial roots along their stems—these anchor them as they climb, and root if they touch soil.

PLANT CARE. The main cultural requirement for an indoor ivy plant is cool temperature. It simply won't perform well in warm rooms above 65° to 70°F (19° to 21°C) or where the temperature fluctuates widely. During ivy's winter rest period, try to find an even cooler spot—close to 50°F/10°C for a few weeks. In all seasons, raise the humidity around the foliage if the air is dry. High temperatures and dry air encourage pests and diseases; they also cause dry, brittle foliage. If your house gets fairly warm, ivy probably won't grow well for you.

Bright reflected or filtered light is best for green-leafed ivies, which tolerate direct sun only in winter; variegated types, however, may lose their distinguishing coloration without 2 to 3 hours of sun a day. In light that's too dim, few leaves develop and stems appear stringy. Use a standard indoor potting mix; allow the top 1 to 2 inches to dry out before moistening thoroughly. Fertilize during active growth with low doses of a balanced fertilizer. Vigorous under the right conditions, ivy falters when stressed. You may be able to avoid problems and invigorate your ivy by summering it out-of-doors in the shade. Common pests include red spider mites, thrips, aphids, and scale; fungal diseases also occur.

SPECIES AND VARIETIES. The most satisfying indoor ivies are those that branch naturally along the stems rather than send out long, vining trailers. Variegated forms add splendid spots of color to nearly any decor. The following small-leafed forms of *Hedera helix* are especially pretty indoors.

'Adam' is mottled in grayish green with a creamy white variegation that yellows as the three-lobed leaves mature. 'Fluffy Ruffles' is popular for its small, five-lobed, medium green leaves with wavy margins. 'Glacier' is a grayish green bordered in white; its leaves have three to five lobes.

HOYA
(HOY-uh)
HINDU ROPE PLANT, PORCELAIN FLOWER, WAX PLANT
Asclepiadaceae

🌿 If you're less than satisfied with the number of blossoms on your hoya, use a high-potassium fertilizer such as 0-10-10 to boost flowering.

O ver 200 species of *Hoya* lure collectors toward this fascinating group of tropical plants. Looking quite exotic with their waxy blossoms and fleshy, leathery foliage, hoyas are old-fashioned favorites among houseplant fanciers and surprisingly easy to care for. Their growth habit varies from wiry vines to shrubby forms, and some have unusual foliage—frosted, fuzzy, reflexed, or succulent. Clusters of long-lasting, star-shaped blossoms appear at leaf nodes in summer; most are sweetly fragrant.

Train twining hoyas on wire rounds, against trellises, or up posts. Use the smaller forms, such as *H. bella,* in hanging baskets. Protect the short stalks that bear flowers; these are long-lived and should never be removed or you will sacrifice blooms. Mature plants produce large clusters in ever-increasing numbers.

PLANT CARE. For decades, hoyas were trained around the sides of sunny kitchen windows. Though this style of display is now out of fashion, that image should remind you of the kind of bright light—some direct, some indirect—that hoyas need to thrive. Give them average room temperatures and

Hoya carnosa

high humidity. Plant them in a fast-draining potting mix that will stay damp but not soggy; allow the soil to dry slightly between waterings. During the winter rest period, the soil should dry nearly completely before you rewater. Fertilize lightly every other week during active growth with a complete fertilizer. Hoya blooms best when pot-bound; therefore, top-dress rather than repot once plants have moved up to a 6- to 8-inch container. Stems root easily (in 7 to 10 days) from cuttings taken in spring when set in water or in a plant-rooting mix.

SPECIES AND VARIETIES. *Hoya australis* has dark green, rounded leaves that are pointed at the end. A fast-growing vine, it produces dense clusters of white flowers. The variety 'Bronze' has shiny green foliage and bronze buds that open to rose-tinted, cream-colored blossoms. 'Variegata' has foliage edged in creamy white; its flowers are blushed a pinkish red.

H. bella is a shrubby, dwarf, small-leafed plant to 3 feet with upright branches that droop as they grow older. White, purple-centered, ½-inch flowers appear in tight clusters; this one is attractive in a hanging basket.

H. carnosa is a vine to 10 feet long, with oval leaves 2 to 4 inches long. Its fragrant summer flowers are creamy white centered with a pink star; its red juvenile leaves add extra color. This species can tolerate low temperatures, but not below freezing.

Hoya carnosa 'Variegata'

Hypoestes phyllostachya

This fast-growing foliage plant from southern Africa can be grown out-of-doors as a summer annual for zesty color spots in beds and borders. Indoors, include it with solid green foliage plants in dish and basket gardens, or place pots of it wherever you want splashes of color. Irregular pink spots (the polka dots) brighten the tops of medium green, 2- to 3-inch oval leaves.

HYPOESTES
(hye-poe-ESS-tees)
FLAMINGO PLANT, FRECKLE FACE, POLKA-DOT PLANT
Acanthaceae

❧ The purple flower spikes detract from the more attractive *Hypoestes* foliage. Remove them as they appear to keep your plants good-looking and vigorously growing.

PLANT CARE. Direct sun brings out the best color in hypoestes foliage, whereas low light reduces the polka-dot effect. Average room temperatures (never below 60°F/16°C), moderate humidity levels, low doses of fertilizer monthly, and constantly moist soil promote rich-looking foliage. In winter, discontinue the fertilizer and allow the top of the soil to dry between waterings.

Keep plants in small pots (5 to 6 inches in diameter), pruning the roots when they become too congested. Pinch off the stem tips to promote fullness. In early spring, cut 1- to 2-foot-high plants down to an inch or so above the soil to completely renew them. During their second or third year, root stem cuttings in water or sow seed for new plants. (Plants become woody and need replacing every few years.) Watch for mealybugs, red spider mites, scale, and whiteflies—especially on potted plants that you set outside for the summer.

SPECIES AND VARIETIES. *Hypoestes phyllostachya*, the most commonly available species, has several popular cultivars. The leaves of 'Carmina' are bright red; 'Purpuriana' has plum-colored foliage; 'Splash' has showier pink spots; and 'Wit' is marbled in white.

RICH REWARDS

Taking the time to draw tepid water or heat it to room temperature before watering or misting your plants will pay off in the long run. Cold water accidentally splashed on foliage or sprayed on when you mist can cause disfiguring brown spots. Cold water on roots can actually shock plants, slow growth, and—on some species—also cause leaf spots. Tepid water, on the other hand, never shocks plants and is safe on foliage.

HERBS INDOORS

Pots of culinary and aromatic herbs make perfect houseplants for the kitchen. You can grow sun-loving Mediterranean herbs in a greenhouse window or on windowsills where they'll get a minimum of 6 hours of sun per day; set more tender types like chervil and ginger in partially shaded spots on countertops. But don't despair if your sun exposure is inadequate; many herbs grow quite successfully under artificial lights. Here are a few tips for growing herbs as houseplants.

❧ Use a soil-based planting mix and fertilize monthly with half-strength doses of a liquid product. Allow the soil to partially dry before rewatering when growing marjoram, oregano, parsley, rosemary, sage, and thyme; keep the soil moist for basil, chervil, chives, ginger, and mint.

❧ Pay attention to the temperature inside a sunny window; for a few weeks in winter, sun-loving herbs need temperatures in the 55° to 65°F (13° to 19°C) range. They can tolerate warmer temperatures during other seasons, so long as the soil doesn't dry out completely.

❧ Rotate containers in windows regularly, in the same direction every time, to promote fairly even growth all around.

❧ Herbs under 40-watt fluorescent tubes need 12 to 14 hours of light per day— roughly the equivalent of 6 hours of sunlight.

Golden sage

IRESINE
(ir-uh-SYE-nee)
BEEFSTEAK PLANT, BEET PLANT,
BLOODLEAF PLANT, CHICKEN
GIZZARD PLANT
Amaranthaceae

❧ Take tip cuttings in late summer if you want extra plants next year to set outside in pots or borders as summer annuals.

This native of dry regions in Brazil and Australia is loved for its intensely hued, purplish red foliage accented by glowing pink midribs and veins; some varieties have bronzy green foliage with yellow highlights. These shrubby plants grow 1 to 2 feet tall; the 1- to 2-inch waxy leaves are oval to round, somewhat puckered and succulent, and notched at the tips. The flowers are insignificant. Once popular in Victorian bedding designs, iresine attains its most intense color in summer.

PLANT CARE. Bright reflected light (2 to 3 hours of direct sun daily) promotes the sharpest leaf color. Moderate

Iresine

humidity levels and temperatures year-round (never below 60°F/16°C) are needed to support healthy foliage. Apply light doses of a balanced fertilizer in spring and summer only; water sparingly in winter. Use a soil-based potting mix. Repot plants once or twice until they become too woody or lose their shape; then replace them. Pinch the growing tips if you want fuller plants. Stem cuttings root readily in either water or a rooting medium.

SPECIES AND VARIETIES. *Iresine herbstii* is an old-fashioned favorite and still the most commonly available species. 'Acuminata' (or 'Versicolor') has sharply pointed, blood red leaves marked with lilac pink. The leaves of 'Aureoreticulata' are apple green with yellow veins; 'Brilliantissima' is crimson; and 'Wallisii' is a dark purple dwarf.

I ndoor gardeners with sunrooms have the perfect location for kohlerias. These plants from the tropical Americas love warm, sunny sites, where they bloom and grow best. In ideal conditions, kohlerias produce numerous rhizomes, each of which sends up a hairy stem with masses of velvety foliage and curiously spotted tubular flowers. The fuzzy blooms—flared at the opening and usually colored pinkish red or white—are kohleria's main feature; they are beautifully shown off on hanging plants.

PLANT CARE. For continuous bloom, kohlerias must have bright light with a few hours of direct sun each day in the morning or late afternoon (midday sun is too strong). Average room temperatures are adequate, but kohlerias really thrive when the daytime temperature rises to 80°F/27°C and then dips 5° to 10°F (3° to 6°C) at night. Below 50°F/10°C, plants lose their foliage and become dormant.

During their active growth and bloom periods, kohlerias like moist soil. Do be sure to test for moisture before watering, but wait until the top ½ to 1 inch of the potting mix is dry. After bloom, keep the soil just lightly moist for 2 to 3 weeks; then resume moderate watering. If you allow the plants to go dormant, reduce your watering even further to prevent the rhizomes from rotting. Fertilize weekly, with quarter-strength doses of liquid fertilizer, during periods of growth and bloom only.

Separate the rhizomes of dormant plants in the spring; on everblooming types, cut back the stems and separate the rhizomes after flowering. Repot as needed, in a soilless mix with extra peat added to retain moisture. Water the dormant rhizomes lightly until sufficient foliage emerges to indicate active growth. Watch for aphids on new growth; thrips may damage the blossoms.

SPECIES AND VARIETIES. You can purchase less common *Kohleria* species from specialty plant growers, but many hybrid crosses are more readily available.

KOHLERIA
(koe-LEER-ee-uh)
TREE GLOXINIA
Gesneriaceae

❧ Move your blooming kohleria into position in a sunless room as a centerpiece for a special event; then return it to its normal bright, humid environment.

Kohleria

M aranta naturally combines colors quite daringly—bright satiny green, chartreuse, vibrant red, silver, and brownish green—to create intricate patterns and sensational foliage displays. At night, its leaves fold together resembling praying hands (a natural technique for conserving moisture), which accounts for one of its common names. The leaves may be up to 8 inches long and 4 inches wide; any flowers are insignificant.

PLANT CARE. Maranta likes a position in bright reflected light away from direct sun, which causes the leaves to scorch or curl and dry. Cool room temperatures—about 65° to 70°F (19° to 21°C)—are ideal; below 55°F/13°C, plants will not flourish. In warmer conditions, increase the humidity to keep the foliage lush and vibrant. Give them plentiful water and regular fertilizer during active growth, but reduce the amount and frequency of both in the late fall and winter while the plants rest; at that time, water only when the top half of the potting mix is dry. Maranta foliage is sensitive to hard water.

You can propagate marantas by taking stem cuttings or making divisions in the spring. Plant them in shallow pots (to match their shallow roots) in a soil-based medium.

SPECIES AND VARIETIES. *Maranta leuconeura* is the most common species; markings on the long, elliptical leaves vary considerably from plant to plant but include zones of dark green, gray, or maroon with silver, red, or purple veining.

M. l. kerchoviana—called rabbit's foot—has grayish green leaves marked with pairs of purplish blotches on either side of the midrib, like a rabbit's tracks.

Maranta leuconeura

MARANTA
(muh-RAN-tuh)
ARROWROOT, PRAYER PLANT, RABBIT'S FOOT, RABBIT'S TRACKS
Marantaceae

❧ If your maranta's leaves regularly fold up at night and open again the next day, rest assured that it has sufficient light for healthy growth. If its leaves stay closed most of the time, move the plant into brighter light.

MONSTERA
(mon-STAIR-uh)
SPLIT-LEAF PHILODENDRON
Araceae

❧ Under ideal conditions monstera flowers and sets fruit, which is not only edible but delicious when fully ripe.

Truly colossal in size, *Monstera* has bright to dark green, heart-shaped foliage that is solid in youth but deeply split—appearing to be scissored into many segments—in maturity. The shape of the 18-inch leaves and the vining habit recall in many ways a large *Philodendron*. This stout-stemmed tropical climber puts out fleshy, cordlike aerial roots that hold onto tree bark and absorb nutrients in rain forests; moss-covered poles provide the "trees" for houseplants. Be prepared to either cut back the vines or enjoy monstrous plants: 15-foot heights are common indoors.

Monstera deliciosa

PLANT CARE. Direct sun in winter and bright reflected light the rest of the year is ideal for monstera. In dim light, its foliage will be small and widely spaced on long, droopy leafstalks. Give your plant average or warmer room temperatures throughout spring and summer (as the room warms, raise the humidity) and cooler—chilly, but frost-free—conditions in fall and winter. When monstera is in a cool environment, its needs diminish: withhold fertilizer and apply water sparingly—just enough to keep the potting mix barely moist. In spring and summer, water more liberally and fertilize lightly every month. Repot young plants annually; top-dress mature ones. Use a moisture-retentive, soil-based potting medium. Propagate by air layering or by rooting cuttings. Scale and spider mites are occasional problems.

SPECIES AND VARIETIES. *Monstera deliciosa* is the most commonly available type. The foliage of 'Albovariegata' has irregular patches of clear white; splashes on 'Variegata' are creamy yellow.

MUSA
(MEW-zuh)
BANANA
Musaceae

❧ Harvest your homegrown bananas cautiously; though they may be edible, they aren't always tasty.

Musa uranoscopus

Giant plants by any measure, the bananas seem even larger indoors. Species vary enormously in size, but few homes can accommodate those with leaves larger than 5 feet long and a foot wide. For dramatic impact, sculptural effect, and frivolous fun, however, it's hard to beat a banana!

PLANT CARE. Bright light with protection from midday sun, ample water, and monthly fertilizing are needed in spring and summer for vigorous growth and healthy foliage. In autumn and winter, keep the soil barely moist and withhold fertilizer while the plants rest. Bananas need a humus-rich, soil-based potting mix and annual top dressing; repot them every other year. Underground rhizomes produce thick clumps of suckering, stemlike leaf sheaths that need dividing every 3 to 5 years. Watch for spider mites, mealybugs, and aphids as well as for disfiguring fungal spots on leaves.

SPECIES AND VARIETIES. *Musa acuminata,* sometimes called the dwarf lady finger banana, can reach 6 to 8 feet indoors, with leaves to 5 feet long. Large, heavy flower clusters appear with reddish to dark purple bracts and yellow flowers. The 3-inch-long bananas are not edible; 'Dwarf Cavendish', however, produces edible fruit. 'Rojo', a blood banana, has red tones on the foliage undersides and the stems.

M. uranoscopus (or *M. coccinea*), red banana, produces glossy, reddish green leaves that reach 2½ feet by 1 foot atop 3-foot "false stems," or leaf sheaths; the yellowish green flowers are surrounded by magenta bracts. 'Red Jamaican' is a prized dwarf variety.

M. velutina is one of the smallest and most desirable ornamental bananas at 3 to 4 feet with 3-foot leaves. The foliage, on yellowish to purplish green stems, is dark green above and paler beneath. It flaunts bright pink bracts, orange flowers, and pink fruit.

Orchids vary so widely that many species and cultivars are unrecognizable members of this huge family of plants. They come in every color except true black, range from tiny miniatures to towering giants, and grow indoors in soil or bark. In nature, terrestrial orchids grow in the ground; epiphytic orchids live in trees or on other plants; and lithophytes live on rocky ledges. Because of their need to hold on and to scavenge for nutrients and moisture, some orchids have evolved fleshy roots and "pseudobulbs" that are often visible on potted plants.

PLANT CARE

At one time, orchids were considered too delicate to be grown outside of a greenhouse. Today, an overwhelming number are available for indoor gardens, though the majority still do best under glass. Those described below are good candidates for typical houseplant culture. For more detailed information on orchid species and care, see the *Sunset* book *Orchids*.

LIGHT AND AIR. Inadequate light is the chief reason for an orchid's failure to bloom. Learn the basic needs of your particular orchid species or cultivar, because some require full sunlight and others need restricted light to perform well. Where light is insufficient, you can add fluorescent lamps that provide a full spectrum of light waves. All orchids need good air circulation, but not drafts; they should be positioned away from heat registers and air conditioning ducts.

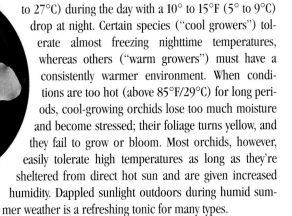

Phalaenopsis

TEMPERATURE AND HUMIDITY. In general, orchids thrive in average room temperatures—70° to 80°F (21° to 27°C) during the day with a 10° to 15°F (5° to 9°C) drop at night. Certain species ("cool growers") tolerate almost freezing nighttime temperatures, whereas others ("warm growers") must have a consistently warmer environment. When conditions are too hot (above 85°F/29°C) for long periods, cool-growing orchids lose too much moisture and become stressed; their foliage turns yellow, and they fail to grow or bloom. Most orchids, however, easily tolerate high temperatures as long as they're sheltered from direct hot sun and are given increased humidity. Dappled sunlight outdoors during humid summer weather is a refreshing tonic for many types.

Paphiopedilum 'Albion'

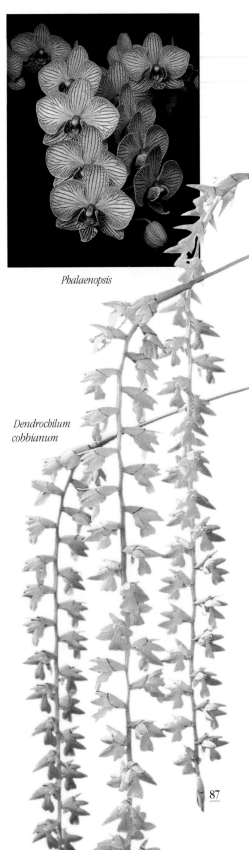

Dendrochilum cobbianum

SOIL AND CONTAINERS. The optimal time to repot orchids is during the 2 to 6 weeks after their blooms have faded. Keep in mind that most thrive and produce superior blossoms when their roots are slightly crowded. Nonetheless, mature plants will need repotting every few years when they outgrow their containers and when the bark in their planting medium has begun to disintegrate. Most epiphytic orchids do best potted in fir bark, but you can also use coconut fiber, vermiculite, and osmunda (the roots of a fern species)—all of which retain moisture yet provide drainage; use lava rock, gravel, and perlite in mixes to further improve drainage. Sphagnum moss and tree fern fiber are useful in maintaining surface moisture for delicate roots and for packing around the roots of orchids mounted on trees or bark slabs.

Some orchids grow and bloom spectacularly when they're fastened against bark, and many do well in a basket of sphagnum moss, but indoors most are grown in pots. Unglazed clay pots have the advantage of allowing air movement around the roots while providing weight that keeps top-heavy plants from falling over. Special pots with slotted or pierced sides provide even greater aeration, as well as faster drainage. Plastic and

Saucers do a great job of catching runoff under pots, but they can be hard to empty if your containers are large and heavy. You can remove excess water that collects in the saucers without handling the pots at all: simply siphon it out with a kitchen bulb baster. About 30 minutes after watering, take a baster and a small pail along as you check for excess water sitting in saucers; siphon the standing water into the plastic baster and empty it into your pail. Plants stay healthier when their pots are well drained.

Cattleya 'Admore'

paper pulp containers can also be used for orchids, though they're not always attractive; you may want to camouflage these in a more decorative glazed container. Check all orchids after watering them to be sure the pots are not sitting in water.

WATER AND FERTILIZER. Most orchids need water once or twice a week, but as with other houseplants, each individual is different and must be watered on demand rather than on schedule. Container size and type, the potting medium, room temperature, humidity, the time of year—all of these factors influence the amount and frequency of watering. One thing you can be sure of: overwatering is worse than underwatering. Orchids have their own water reservoirs in their thickened roots and leaves, so they can stay on the dry side for a few days without suffering. If at all possible, use rainwater; never use soft water from a sodium-exchange water softener.

A *Paphiopedilum* hybrid

Orchids that are fed frequently with a complete fertilizer grow fastest. Use a high-nitrogen product (for instance, one formulated with a 3-1-1 ratio) for orchids growing in bark; use a 1-1-1 formula for those growing in other media. You may want to substitute a special bloom formula (1-3-2) when growth is complete and flower buds are about to form. Apply a fertilizer solution in half-strength doses every week while orchids are actively growing, once every 2 weeks while they are at rest.

PESTS AND DISEASES. Thankfully, orchids have few pests. When insects do appear, physically remove them or spray with a mild soap. For more serious infestations use a botanical pesticide or, if all else fails, a chemical control. Isolate any infected plant until the problem clears up. Remove and destroy diseased plant parts, sterilizing your cutting tool after each cut with rubbing alcohol or bleach. Treat the cut surface with a fungicide formulated specifically for orchids, available from nurseries or orchid suppliers.

SPECIES AND VARIETIES

As is true of other large plant families, there are many ways to classify orchids. Societies and growers divide them into "alliances"—groups of related genera that are similar in appearance and in cultural needs. Many of these interbreed freely, leading to an astounding number of cultivated varieties. Many new ones appear each year.

CATTLEYA (KAT-lee-uh). The cattleya alliance is a good starting place for beginning orchid growers. Many of the cultivars available today are complex hybrids, and they number into the thousands. The various species differ somewhat in their cultural needs, so when you purchase a cattleya, ask what conditions it prefers—sun or filtered light, warm or cool temperatures. (Happily, most are tolerant of wide extremes.) An intermediate range from 70° to 75°F (21° to 24°C) in the daytime and 55° to 60°F (13° to 16°C) at night is ideal; at higher temperatures, increase the humidity level and be sure to provide good air circulation. When potting this group's orchids, use a bark or a bark-perlite potting mixture and containers small enough to restrict root growth (the plants bloom better when their roots are confined). Water freely in warm conditions, when plants are actively growing; reduce watering in winter. Never allow pots to sit in water; the bark should dry out before rewatering.

Cattleya. The namesakes of this large alliance, these are the showy blooms so popular in corsages and the origin of the classic purple hue that we call orchid. Newer varieties have introduced white, pale pink, and yellow as well as deeper hues: orange, red, deep purple, and green. The blooms of some species are marked with spots and stripes; others are flushed with bronze and dark green.

Epidendrum. Many, but not all, plants in this group develop flower stems on thickened pseudobulbs that arise from the rhizome. Buds form late in the year, but blossoming usually doesn't begin until the following spring. Others, such as *Epidendrum ibaguense* and its hybrids (known as reed-stem epidendrums), lack a pseudobulb but flower nearly continuously on slender canes that can reach 2 to 4 feet indoors. Epidendrums with canelike stems are often terrestrial plants, so they can be grown in a soil-based potting mix.

Laelia. Closely related to *Cattleya,* many species in this genus must endure long, dry periods in their native habitats; some attach themselves to trees and others grow on rocks. *Laelia anceps* and *L. autumnalis* are hardy enough to grow out-of-doors in mild climates (where temperatures seldom drop below freezing).

TOP: *Epidendrum stanfordianum*
BOTTOM: × *Laeliocattleya* 'Mauvine Gloaming'

Cymbidium 'Tom Thumb'

CYMBIDIUM (sim-BID-ee-uhm). Given the right conditions, these orchids are among the easiest to grow. Standard hybrids bloom for long periods in late winter through spring; flowering is heavy, with as many as thirty 4- to 5-inch blossoms on stems up to 4 feet tall. Some smaller-growing and dwarf species produce dangling flower spikes. All types have long, narrow, grasslike leaves that form a sheath around a stout, oval pseudobulb. The long-lasting flowers, like those of cattleyas, are popular for corsages.

In order to set flower buds, cymbidiums must have nighttime temperatures below 60°F/16°C in the fall. During their growth period, spring through fall, they require more water than they do in winter. Even though they may grow in the ground naturally, cymbidiums should be planted in fine-grade fir bark blended with peat moss, leaf mold, or perlite. Whereas many other types of orchids benefit from the weight of a clay pot, cymbidiums' heavy root balls make them easier to handle in plastic pots.

Miniature cymbidiums are dainty, petite versions that bloom profusely in the same color range as that of the standards: white, pink, red, bronze, brown, yellow, and green—usually with contrasting lips. They tend to begin their bloom in summer.

DENDROBIUM (den-DROE-bee-uhm). This alliance is highly variable in both size and appearance, containing species nearly microscopic as well as those over 10 feet tall, in nearly every color tone and combination of hues. Their cultural requirements also vary depending on a species' origin—warm or cool climate, tropical rain forest, rocky highland, or pine forest. Some dendrobiums develop pseudobulbs, but most have canelike stems. Cool-growing types are deciduous and require a dry winter rest; warm-growing species are generally evergreen and need more moisture. Many produce dense floral clusters.

ONCIDIUM (on-SID-ee-uhm). Fascinating flowers decorate this alliance, many the result of interbreeding among various genera and species, and ongoing study has led to some species gaining new names. These orchids are native to diverse environments, exhibit various forms, and bloom at different times of the year. In general, however, they require the same care as do the cattleyas.

Brassia. Commonly called spider orchids, these plants have appropriately long-legged blossoms. Some are huge; those of *Brassia gireoudiana,* for instance, are 10 to 12 inches across.

Dendrobium densiflorum

TOP: *Oncidium ornithorhynchum*
BOTTOM: *Lemboglossum rossii*
(*Oncidium* alliance)

Oncidium. This genus includes hundreds of species from the tropical Americas, a few as far north as Florida. Their flared petals are generally borne in branching sprays in shades of yellow, red, white, or pink; they are lovely in cut-flower arrangements. The foliage is broad, sometimes in a fanlike arrangement similar to that of an iris. It's a good idea to ask about specific care requirements for these orchids, because the species' origins differ so much.

VANDA (VAN-duh). Plants in this orchid alliance include several genera and hybrid crosses. Lacking moisture-storing pseudobulbs, they instead have evolved thick leaves and roots that allow them to withstand some drying out. True to their tropical origins, they love heat and light. Well loved and widely grown, vandas are among the showiest of all houseplants.

Vanda coerulea

Phalaenopsis. Called the moth orchid, phalaenopsis is tolerant of low light and average household conditions; it's a good choice for beginners and very widely available. The leaves are always attractive: wide and plump, shiny, deep green or mottled. Some plants seem to bloom nearly continuously. Repot moth orchids every year or so to replace the bark potting medium, which breaks down fairly rapidly. Expect the roots to grow above as well as within the potting medium; mist them and the foliage frequently. Keep the bark moist, but never allow pots to sit in water, or the roots and leaves will rot. After bloom, cut the flower stem just below where the first flower appeared; a second stem may produce additional blossoms. Most plants for sale are hybrids.

Vanda. These are generally large plants that need plenty of indoor space for their vertically expanding stems and strap-shaped foliage. Their leaves are arranged in opposite ranks, and aerial roots form along the stem. These orchids bloom best when they receive bright light and high humidity year-round. *Vanda coerulea* is a favorite that produces long-lasting blue flowers from fall to spring.

OTHER ORCHIDS. Not all orchids fit neatly into alliances. Many are classified by their botanical name alone, others known by their growth habits and unusual flowers. The following notable groups cannot be left out.

Botanicals. Orchids once considered mere botanical curiosities are slowly drifting into the wider world of houseplants. Gardeners new to orchid growing may want to try a *Coelogyne,* a rain forest epiphyte; a compact and highly perfumed *Dendrochilum,* with long, trailing wands of tiny flowers; or a tiger-striped *Zygopetalum.*

Zygopetalum

Slipper orchids. Unique among the orchid family, these plants have fascinating, pouchlike blossoms that suggest the shape of a tiny lady's slipper. The thick, waxy blooms are usually borne singly on new growth only, though the plants themselves may live for many years. Most of the favorites are included in the *Paphiopedilum* genus, which includes largely cool-climate, terrestrial orchids. Because they lack pseudobulbs, these orchids need constant moisture. Otherwise, they accept typical orchid culture, but it must be meticulously carried out. Two important cautions: never use softened water containing salts, and never water late in the day; salts can be fatal, and standing water in the foliage encourages decay.

Coelogyne cristata

U nrivaled for elegance, palms have been decorating parlors and living rooms for the last century or so. These plants add a natural grace to almost any interior that has room for an oversize pot and broad, arching fronds. Though many mature palms planted in the ground have tall, cylindrical, and stout trunks, as houseplants these trees usually remain in their juvenile phase; substantial trunks rarely form. In fact, indoor palms are slow growing and shrublike, producing only two or three new leaves, or fronds, each year.

Palm fronds are usually divided into many smaller, narrower segments. Fan palms have leaflets that radiate, fanlike, from their base; in other types, leaflets are arranged feather-fashion along a long, central stem. When you select a palm, be sure to choose a variety whose structure and growth habit will fit your indoor space. If you try to top-prune a palm to restrict its growth, it will die.

PLANT CARE

In general, palms are subtropical or tropical in origin and therefore thrive in warm, humid conditions. Most, however, aren't too fussy about their requirements.

LIGHT. In the wild, mature palms grow in full sun, but young ones usually start out under the shelter of a high canopy of taller shrubs and trees. Because most palms indoors never really mature, they grow best in similarly bright filtered or dappled light; many also tolerate and benefit from 1 to 3 hours of morning or late-afternoon (not midday) sun daily. Though they'll survive in low-light environments, they won't thrive without some exposure to sun or bright light.

WATER, TEMPERATURE, AND HUMIDITY. As a rule, palms should be given enough water during their active growth in spring and summer to saturate the soil, but their pots should never sit in water. During cool seasons, reduce room temperature and allow the soil to dry almost completely; then water lightly. As temperatures rise, you'll want to increase the humidity and water more heavily to maintain the appearance of the foliage. Although palms do tolerate average to dry air, frond tips will brown if the humidity is too low.

SOIL AND FERTILIZER. Palms do best in a potting mix that retains water yet has excellent drainage. If you use a soilless medium, fertilize monthly during spring and summer with the recommended dose of a commercial product; use half-stength doses for palms in a soil-based mix. Withhold fertilizer in autumn and winter until active growth resumes. Repot every few years or as needed to prevent compacted roots; choose a container just slightly larger than the one your palm is in. Take care to avoid damaging the thick, fleshy roots that some species have. When you repot, leave ample space at the top of the pot to allow for the development of these roots, which push the root ball toward the top of the container over time.

PESTS AND DISEASES. Dust-free foliage helps keep palms vigorous and protects them against spider mites. Hand-wash large plants; give regular showers to those you can easily move. Palms resist most insect attacks, but may be bothered by mites and scale. Fungal leaf spots sometimes appear.

SPECIES AND VARIETIES

The following eight palm groups are longtime favorites; a few have special cultural requirements. Though there are many other palms, these are some of the easiest to grow in most indoor situations. If you're planning to purchase a palm, keep in mind that large palms are usually quite expensive and that a smaller one— though less dramatic initially—can be nurtured to a good size at a much lower cost.

PALMS AND PALMLIKE PLANTS

Caryota

Chrysalidocarpus lutescens

91

CARYOTA (kah-ree-OE-tuh). The uniquely shaped leaflets of the fishtail palm are split into wedge-shaped sections and flattened at their tips, like fish tails. Caryotas grow slowly (3 to 5 inches per year), but eventually they'll reach 8 feet.

Caryota mitis, clustered fishtail palm, slowly develops multiple trunks and light green leaflets. Each year or two, the oldest frond usually yellows and dies. You can make new plants by separating basal offshoots that are 1 foot tall and rooting them further in a soil-based potting medium. As the root mass increases, move them to a larger pot.

CHAMAEDOREA (kam-ee-DOR-ee-uh). These relatively short, feathery-leafed palms are among the easiest to grow. Always graceful and never imposing, they seldom exceed 3 to 4 feet indoors. Canelike stems may be single or may appear in clusters. Keep these palms out of direct sun, to prevent scorching.

Chamaedorea costaricana grows quickly under ideal conditions into bamboolike, narrowly upright clumps of eight to ten trunks. Individual leaflets are narrow, imparting a lacy look.

C. elegans, parlor palm, is often sold as *Neanthe bella.* It tolerates crowded roots, low light, and dry air; you may need to trim off brown frond tips if the humidity is too low. 'Bella' is a miniature and one of the most popular of all houseplants.

CHRYSALIDOCARPUS (cri-SAL-luh-do-KAHR-pus). Widely sold in clumps of several stems, *Chrysalidocarpus lutescens* (or *Areca lutescens*) epitomizes the charm of an indoor palm. Its appeal lies in the delicate, arching sprays of its featherlike fronds. As they increase in height, the fronds give these plants an upright yet layered appearance. Young stems are reedy, mature ones more canelike and similar to bamboo. The stems' yellow color accounts for the plant's common name of yellow palm; it's also called butterfly palm. Although these palms grow at a moderate rate, they eventually become too large for indoor use.

HOWEA (HOW-ee-uh). Parlor palms of yesteryear, these natives of Lord Howe Island in the South Pacific are still sold today, usually as kentia palm. Their large, feathery leaves assume the classic profile associated with the Victorian parlor. With age, old leaves drop off to reveal a smooth green stem ringed with leaf scars. Howea tolerates a wide range of indoor conditions, withstanding low light, low humidity, and general neglect.

Howea belmoreana, sentry palm or curly palm, develops a thickened base and short trunk. The smaller and more compact of the two *Howea* species, it will ultimately reach 6 to 7 feet high by 6 feet wide.

Howea

H. forsteriana, paradise palm, is larger overall than sentry palm, though no trunk develops. Its mature fronds may become 3 feet long; the leaflets are wider spaced (to 1 inch apart) and longer, which accounts for the more graceful, draping appearance of this species. You can expect a 10-foot spread on an 8-foot plant.

PHOENIX (FEE-nix). These naturally large palm trees would normally be excluded from indoor gardens if it weren't for their exquisitely beautiful and refined nature in youth. They are slow growing enough to stay in bounds for several years, qualifying them for container culture. Individual plants may vary widely.

Phoenix canariensis, the Canary Island date palm, looks very much like a pineapple when young. Its feathery fronds arch stiffly—but after several years, they become quite long as the plants grow too large for indoor culture.

P. roebelinii, known as the miniature date palm, is more willowy than the other types, yet just as durable. Dark green, finely divided, arching fronds rise from a slightly

Chamaedorea elegans

Phoenix roebelinii

bulbous base. The fronds may reach 2 feet in length and spread twice as wide on plants that are seldom more than 3 feet tall. To maintain the graceful appearance of a single-stemmed plant, remove suckering offsets as they appear around the base; you can combine those small, fernlike palms with other plants in a dish garden.

RHAPIS (RAP-uhs). One of the finest clump-forming fan palms, the lady palm grows slowly and almost never gets too big for indoor display; it also manages to survive considerable neglect. The trunk is covered with a netted, dark green, fibrous leaf sheath, which is shed in sections when a leafstalk drops. Keep plants in small pots to restrict their size. This palm likes even moisture, so you can put it in a self-watering container.

Rhapis excelsa, also called bamboo palm, has thickened stems up to an inch in diameter that support thin leafstalks, each bearing three to ten slightly puckered, blunt-tipped leaflets. 'Variegata' and other variegated forms have white markings.

R. humilis is called slender lady palm or reed palm for its thin, reedy stems. This palm grows taller (to 8 feet indoors). The stem fibers are less coarse and the leaflets longer, more numerous, and rounded, giving this species a lusher, more graceful look. It tolerates low light exceptionally well.

Rhapis excelsa

Nothing looks quite so cheerful and homey as a potted geranium growing happily on a sunny windowsill. Whether it enjoys frequent grooming or long-term neglect, this agreeable plant knows how to satisfy. The wide-ranging *Pelargonium* group includes a great diversity of flower and leaf forms. The appeal of some species resides in the hue or scent of their foliage; others are grown strictly for their winsome blossoms; all bloom in white or shades of pink, rose, red, and purple. Of the vast number of species and cultivars awaiting both the casual and serious gardener, nearly all hide a rugged nature beneath their outer charm.

PLANT CARE. This is one plant that not only tolerates unfiltered sun but depends on it. Give plants at least 4 hours of direct exposure each day; in poor light, flowering wanes and plants lose their vigor. Typical indoor conditions—average room temperatures and normal humidity—suit geraniums very well. Ideally, they should have cooler nights than days. They do benefit from a period of cool rest in winter, with nighttime temperatures in the 50°F/10°C range for several weeks. As a rule, water potted geraniums sparingly, more while they're actively blooming and growing. Always probe for moisture first, and water only when the top half-inch or so of the soil dries out; too much water will do more harm than good. Fertilize regularly during active growth with a formula such as 5-10-10 or 1-6-5; the lower nitrogen content and higher percentages of phosphorus and potassium promote blooming. Use a standard soil-based potting mix.

Potted geraniums are really small shrubs that need pinching when young to encourage bushiness and a low, well-branched shape. You can control the looks of your plants without too much effort by repotting and trimming them each spring; or you can follow the lead of many gardeners who take cuttings to renew plants, discarding older specimens after 1 or 2 years. If you choose to repot, loosen the plants from the potting mix and trim off the longer roots. Cut back the top growth by half, or to 5 inches. Pinch off the growing tips (but not the flower buds) after new stems have reached the desired height.

Geranium leaves die and drop naturally over time. When you find yellowed leaves, however, check your care procedures to be sure that you're not over- or underwatering, that plants are receiving adequate sunlight, and that spider mites are not the problem.

SPECIES AND VARIETIES. Virtually all potted geraniums fall into one of four categories: three are distinct groups of mainly hybrid cultivars and the fourth is a large group of species with aromatic foliage, loosely referred to as the scented geraniums.

PELARGONIUM
(pel-ahr-GOE-nee-uhm)
GERANIUM
Geraniaceae

The houseplant that we commonly call a geranium is botanically classified as a *Pelargonium*. The genus *Geranium* grows out-of-doors only; its members are valuable in perennial borders and rock gardens.

Pelargonium × domesticum 'Princess'

TOP: *Pelargonium × hortorum* 'Mr. Henry Cox'
BOTTOM: *Pelargonium peltatum*

Pelargonium × domesticum, better known as the regal or Martha Washington geranium, has heart- to kidney-shaped, dark green, slightly pleated foliage with toothed and crinkled margins. Brilliantly colored flowers in loose clusters are splashed with darker markings. Plants in this group need a summer rest after the spring and early-summer bloom period. Unlike other geraniums, they should be repotted in autumn rather than spring, and they need temperatures below 60°F/16°C in autumn and winter. Don't be afraid to cut back their stems severely; these are vigorous growers. Whiteflies are a common pest.

P. × hortorum, the bedding or zonal geranium, is highly regarded for its rounded foliage, some with "zones" of cream, red, copper, or green; the leaves are lobed, scalloped, and velvety to the touch. Numerous strains and nearly countless cultivars exist as dwarf, cactus-flowered, star-leafed, miniature, and other forms. Many have beautiful blossoms from spring through autumn. Flowers in this group are smaller individually than those of *P. × domesticum,* but there are more in each cluster. The standard reddish orange geranium often seen on windowsills belongs to this group.

P. peltatum, the ivy geranium, has succulent, glossy, scalloped green leaves that are pointed at the tips. As the common name suggests, these plants have a vining habit and are well suited to hanging baskets and window boxes. Like other geraniums, they become fuller with frequent pinching, though you may want to let several stems lengthen for a cascading effect. Numerous cultivars exist, with diverse habits. Most flower heavily, some with roselike blossoms; others have variegated foliage.

Scented *Pelargoniums* are grown primarily for the delicious aroma they release when their foliage is brushed. Popular fragrances include lemon *(P. crispum),* rose *(P. graveolens),* lime *(P. nervosum),* apple *(P. odoratissimum),* and peppermint *(P. tomentosum);* several other hybrids belong to the *P. × fragrans* group. Many of these plants arch into captivating mounds and are attractive in hanging baskets; most can also be beautifully displayed as miniature topiaries. The leaves may be variegated, toothed, or deeply lobed; the flowers are generally small and single.

Pelargonium graveolens

PEPEROMIA
(pep-uh-ROE-mee-uh)
RADIATOR PLANT
Piperaceae

If you grew only peperomias, you could amass quite a collection from the thousand or so members of this plant group. Their main attraction is the rich diversity of their foliage texture and color. The succulent leaves are predominantly dark green, reddish bronze, or a creamy variegation; they may be smooth, crinkled, or puckered. Most plants grow in low clumps, but a few are vines.

PLANT CARE. Indirect light from a sunny window suits variegated peperomias; light that is too bright can be harmful (and those with solid green foliage must never receive direct sun). All types enjoy average room temperatures year-round, but they will drop their lower leaves if the air is too dry; mist frequently or use humidity trays. Allow the soil to dry out almost completely between waterings; then water lightly. Overwatering causes severe leaf drop and may kill the plants. Except in autumn and winter, apply a half-strength liquid fertilizer monthly. Pests are rarely a problem. Propagate peperomia from tip cuttings or make leaf cuttings from *P. argyreia* and *P. caperata.* These plants tend to be short-lived.

LEFT TO RIGHT: *Peperomia argyreia, P. caperata* 'Emerald Ripple', and *P. obtusifolia*

SPECIES AND VARIETIES. *Peperomia argyreia,* the watermelon peperomia, forms a rosette of nearly round, 3- to 5-inch green leaves pointed at the tip. Gray stripes and long red stems provide color interest.

The foliage of *P. caperata* 'Emerald Ripple' is heart shaped, dark green, and deeply veined to give a rippled effect. The short-stemmed leaves grow in low clumps, above which rise narrow spikes of greenish white flowers; the plants rarely exceed 3 or 4 inches in height. 'Little Fantasy' is similar but even smaller.

P. obtusifolia, a longtime favorite familiarly known as the baby rubber plant, has fleshy, dark green leaves and thick upright or trailing stems to 6 inches.

Philodendron scandens

It's no wonder that the popular, leafy green philodendron is nearly synonymous with the term *houseplant.* These shiny green shrubs and vines are easy to care for and remain good-looking for years on end. The vining types look best swirled around a moss-covered pole or other water-absorbent column that keeps them moist; smaller-leafed specimens can be grown as trailers. "Self-heading" types branch out at their growing tips without pinching or pruning; these develop into short, broad plants with sets of leaves radiating from a very short main stem. Large-leafed species and arborescent versions that can easily fill half a room are more often seen in conservatories than in homes.

PLANT CARE. Philodendrons need only basic care: bright reflected or filtered light (no direct sun), average room temperatures and humidity, moderate amounts of water, a standard potting mix (kept barely moist in winter), and a half-strength liquid fertilizer each month in spring and summer. Though extra humidity does promote healthier foliage, fungal infections can be a problem in excessively moist environments. Insect pests are few, but watch for mealybugs and aphids.

SPECIES AND VARIETIES. *Philodendron bipennifolium,* horsehead or fiddleleaf philodendron, is a fast-growing vining type. Its juvenile heart-shaped leaves become more bulbous, pointed at the tip and lobed at the base, in maturity. This species needs sturdy support.

P. bipinnatifidum is more treelike than vining. Its large, heart-shaped leaves are deeply cut into many segments with wavy margins. Some varieties are more finely cut, larger leafed, or longer stemmed than others. 'Miniature Selloum' is a dwarf with small, thick-stalked leaves. Many of these cultivars are able to withstand low-light conditions.

P. erubescens, red-leaf philodendron, adds red hues to the usual glossy, dark green foliage. Its young stems are reddish purple, the leaf undersides a coppery reddish purple. The related hybrid cultivar 'Burgundy' is considerably slower growing than the species and rarely requires staking. Its smaller leaves are infused with red.

P. scandens, heart-leaf philodendron, is the most common houseplant in this group. The deep green leaves, 5 inches long on most plants, may reach 12 inches in maturity. The young foliage of *P. s. oxycardium* is flushed bronzy brown. Velvety 'Micans' has bronzy red leaves; it easily tolerates low light.

Philodendron cultivars of uncertain parentage are also widely grown. 'Emerald King' has spade-shaped, pointed leaves to 12 inches in length; 'Emerald Queen' is a choice deep green form. 'Red Duchess' displays dark green, heart-shaped leaves on long red stems; its leaf undersides are also red.

☙ Try combining a low tuft of peperomia with an upright sansevieria in a dish garden. Peperomia's spikelike flowers will echo the colors and outline of the taller, stiffer leaves.

PHILODENDRON
(fil-oe-DEN-drun)
Araceae

☙ You'll have better luck training a philodendron to climb a vertical support if you tie the vining stems to it as they grow. Aerial roots that protrude unattractively can be cut off.

Philodendron bipinnatifidum

PILEA

(PYE-lee-uh)
ALUMINUM PLANT, ARTILLERY
PLANT, CREEPING CHARLIE
Urticaceae

Pilea 'Golden Brocade'

☙ Keep these plants in small pots 3 to 4 inches in diameter; *Pilea* has shallow roots and thrives when pot-bound.

Pilea houseplants are grown for their highly colored, glistening, or textured foliage. Individual species vary considerably. Many plants have beautifully patterned, thickened, and succulent leaves, but stems that become leggy or woody with age; plan on replacing these after a few years. You can obtain new plants inexpensively by rooting your own stem cuttings; new plants fill out in just a few months.

Pilea cadierei

PLANT CARE. Pileas grow well in moderate to bright light (no direct sun) in a warm environment—about 70° to 85°F (21° to 29°C). Set your pots on humidity trays to supply extra moisture around the foliage. From spring through early autumn, water moderately and fertilize monthly; allow half of the potting mix to dry out before rewatering. In winter, water just enough to keep some moisture in the soil. Pinch the growing tips to promote fullness; check for mealybugs and spider mites.

SPECIES AND VARIETIES. *Pilea cadierei* is named aluminum plant for the rows of silvery patches up and down its bright green, slightly notched leaves. Repeated pinching of the upright stems results in a denser, more attractive shape.

    P. microphylla, artillery plant, spreads a fine thicket of branches and succulent twigs 6 to 12 inches high and as wide. The tiny, thickly set leaves look very fernlike. Remove the nearly inconspicuous pale flowers before they mature to prevent them from firing a round of pollen a foot or more into the room.

    P. nummularifolia, creeping Charlie, grows rapidly in trailing or creeping fashion. Its round, scalloped leaves look lovely in a hanging basket.

PLECTRANTHUS

(plek-TRAN-thus)
CANDLE PLANT, ROYAL CHARLIE,
SWEDISH IVY
Lamiaceae

☙ Usually seen in hanging baskets, plectranthus can also be planted as a ground cover indoors in a large planter box or atrium. The trailing stems root as they grow.

Plectranthus australis

Amateur indoor gardeners love houseplants belonging to the *Plectranthus* genus—though they may call them by their common names rather than by botanical epithets. These mostly trailing plants are fast growing, quick to please, and popular for hanging baskets. The thickish, pale to medium green leaves have scalloped edges and prominent veins, often in a contrasting color. Small white or bluish flowers (resembling coleus blossoms) borne on spikes may detract from the decorative effect you want to achieve. You can snip them off at any time.

PLANT CARE. Plectranthus favors bright light, though most types will tolerate lower intensities. If you notice pale foliage and stringy stems, move your plants to a brighter exposure that gets a few hours of direct sun each day. Average room temperatures and plentiful watering are the general rule, but there are exceptions. Increase the humidity level as room temperatures rise, and give your plants a cool rest for several weeks in winter—between 50° and 60°F (10° and 16°C). Never let the planting medium become too soggy or sit in water; during the winter rest water sparingly, allowing the soil to become nearly dry. Apply fertilizer in half-strength doses every 2 weeks during active growth.

    As plants age, the fast-growing stems continue to dangle, but they also pile on top of each other to form dense, succulent mounds. If you pinch the stem tips frequently, those mounds will be fuller and more attractive. Don't be reluctant to toss out a straggly specimen; you can easily replace it with a few rooted cuttings (they root in either water or soil), and you'll have a new plant in just several weeks.

SPECIES AND VARIETIES. *Plectranthus australis*—called Swedish ivy, after the gardeners who first cherished it—produces waxy, dark green leaves that are 1½ inches round and scalloped along the margins. Its upright stems bend and trail.

P. forsteri 'Marginatus' is a popular variegated species.

P. oertendahlii, commonly called royal Charlie or candle plant, has small, 1-inch leaves of bronzy green marked with silvery veins and suffused with purple beneath; the edges are purple and scalloped.

Plectranthus forsteri 'Marginatus'

SAINTPAULIA
(saynt-PAW-lee-uh)
AFRICAN VIOLET
Gesneriaceae

It may seem like pampering, but your violets will thank you if you give them tepid water and apply it only to the soil, not the foliage. They also like to have their leaves cleaned with a very soft brush.

Today's African violets are the most popular of all flowering houseplants. They trace their heritage to several species collected in East Africa in the late 19th century, but their appearance today derives from years of intensive hybridization among only a few of the 20 species. Catalogs print exhaustive lists of named cultivars that flaunt a seemingly infinite assortment of flowers and foliage. The velvety leaves may be tailored and symmetrical, quilted and ruffled, or stunningly variegated in white and pink. Flower forms range from buttercups and pansies to bells and stars; they may have fringed or ruffled petals and be single, semidouble, or fully double. (The flowers on the original *Saintpaulia* species plants normally have only five petals—two at the top and three larger ones below.)

The original blue and purple African violets are still happily blooming, but most have yielded the spotlight to new color tones. Modern violets also appear in white (the touchiest sort to grow), all shades of pink, burgundy, and even crimson—the latest rage. Creamy yellows exist, but they have a tendency to revert back to pink or purple; the yellows, which intensify as plants mature, stand out best under artificial light. Some of the fanciest blooms show off bands of color, white frilly edges, contrasting veining, and a spattering of dark accents on paler petals. All have bright yellow centers. Their most outstanding feature is their ability to bloom continuously, or at least abundantly, for much of the year—given, of course, the proper care.

PLANT CARE. Generally, African violets need abundant filtered light. In summer, however, move your plants away from any direct sun to where they will receive less intense, indirect light only. Windows with eastern and western exposures offer the best light, but move plants aside if their foliage begins to scorch. For symmetrical growth turn pots gradually, so that they are rotated completely every month or so. Give violets under artificial light about 12 hours of exposure each day.

Violets like the same comfort level as you do: average room temperatures or a little warmer in the day and a few degrees cooler at night (to 65°F/19°C). Keep the humidity high around your plants by placing them on a humidity tray. Never allow them to sit in water; they will die from fungal rots in soggy conditions. Whenever the top half-inch of the planting mix feels dry to the touch, add enough water to make it evenly moist. Always avoid extremes for best plant health—never too wet and never too dry. Fertilize weekly or at each watering with very light doses of a product formulated for African violets. You might want to try growing violets in self-watering pots to help maintain a balance of moisture and fertilizer.

You can propagate your violets by potting up offsets that appear at the base. (To maintain heavy flowering, these plantlets should be removed whenever they appear—whether or not you keep them.) Use a commercial potting mix formulated for African violets or make your own: use 1 part leaf mold, 1 part sterilized loam, and 1 part builder's (not beach) sand. Add 1 tablespoon of bonemeal per half-gallon of mix. Some gardeners prefer to use mostly leaf mold, to substitute peat for loam, and to include some vermiculite and perlite. Begin potting in small, 3-inch pots and slowly move plants

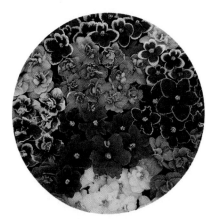

Saintpaulia hybrids

Saintpaulia 'Natalie'

Saintpaulia 'Sunlit Sugar Plum'

into larger sizes as the root mass expands. Far from suffering from pot-bound conditions, African violets actually prefer them, blooming more prolifically with somewhat constricted roots. Always use a shallow pot that is one-third the diameter of the plant. Keep an eye out for aphids, mealybugs, and cyclamen mites.

SPECIES AND VARIETIES. Houseplant lovers usually choose their African violets by flower color and shape, but hybridizers categorize them first of all by size: large, standard, semiminiature, miniature, and microminiature. Among all of these are trailing types that produce rosettes on lengthened stems. Whatever the size, the blossoms are alluring; some have remained irresistible for decades. For example, 'Leila Marie'—a frilly double pink—and 'Spanish Moss'—a variegated-foliage, double two-toned lavender—are two old favorites that are still popular.

Among newer hybrids, 'Ice Fantasy' has star-shaped, double white blooms; 'Juicy' is a double pink with orchid edges; and 'Stuart' has bell-shaped, semidouble purple blossoms. Additions to the growing list of red-blooming cultivars include 'Jeanette', a semidouble fuchsia red ruffled in white; 'Marcella', with star-shaped, single red blossoms edged in white ruffles; and 'Quiet Expression', a deeper rose red with a violet band and white edge.

SAXIFRAGA
(saks-IF-ruh-guh)
MOTHER-OF-THOUSANDS,
STRAWBERRY BEGONIA,
STRAWBERRY GERANIUM
Saxifragaceae

❧ Select a few vigorous plantlets from those that dangle on saxifraga runners to pot up in small containers. Use them to replace 2- to 3-year-old plants as they begin to decline.

Like a strawberry plant, the strawberry begonia (not a begonia at all, but a saxifraga from Asia) produces creeping runners that bear new plantlets. Their profusion accounts for the name mother-of-thousands; the nearly round, white-veined leaves with pink undersides suggest a begonia. The leaves and reddish-stemmed leafstalks bristle with short, soft hairs. These plants mound gently to 8 inches high, but you'll need nearly 3 feet of vertical space to display them: the runners trail as much as 2 feet below the plants, and wiry flower stems wave loose clouds of pendent white flowers up to 12 inches above the foliage mounds.

Saxifraga stolonifera 'Tricolor'

PLANT CARE. Saxifraga grows best when it receives a few hours of direct morning sun and bright light the rest of the day—yet it prefers a cool environment. Where room temperatures are normal or warmer, increase the humidity by misting frequently or using humidity trays. Keep the soil mix evenly moist from spring through autumn, but in winter water only enough to prevent the soil from drying out completely. Fertilize regularly during the months of active growth.

SPECIES AND VARIETIES. *Saxifraga stolonifera* is the only species in this genus that is widely grown as a houseplant. The cultivar 'Tricolor' (or 'Magic Carpet') has rose pink tints sprinkled over cream-colored margins and green leaf centers. This form loses its compact, tuftlike shape unless it receives several hours of direct sun each day.

SCHEFFLERA
(SHEF-luh-ruh)
FALSE ARALIA, OCTOPUS TREE,
UMBRELLA TREE
Araliaceae

Usually seen as a wide-spreading and lofty indoor tree, schefflera grows quickly to a towering 6 to 12 feet (20 feet or more out-of-doors in frost-free climates) and deserves a prominent place of its own. Smaller forms can be used in combination with other plants, but they may be difficult to find. The common name of umbrella tree refers to the way the plant carries its giant, shiny leaves. Borne in horizontal tiers, the long-stalked leaves are split into 7 to 16 leaflets, each up to a foot long; these radiate outward, resembling the segments of an umbrella. Though schefflera may flower outside, it rarely does so indoors.

PLANT CARE. Providing bright light—but not direct sun—is the key to producing dense, glossy foliage on all *Shefflera* species. With moderate moisture, regular light doses of fertilizer, average room temperatures, and ample humidity, these arboreal standouts add leafy freshness to interior decors. Your plant will be most vigorous if it spends some time out-of-doors in warm seasons in a lightly shaded location protected from searing sun. Check for aphids, red spider mites, mealybugs, and scale; dust-free, well-humidified plants suffer the fewest problems.

As its size increases, repot your schefflera into a larger container using a soil-based mix. When you no longer wish to increase pot size, root-prune and top-dress the plant each spring as new growth begins. In fall and winter, hold back on fertilizer and lengthen the intervals between waterings to allow the soil to dry.

SPECIES AND VARIETIES. *Schefflera actinophylla,* the most common indoor species, is often sold as *Brassaia actinophylla.* Hawaiian elf schefflera, *S. arboricola,* is similar but has much smaller leaves. It grows into an interesting sculptural form if you position the root ball so the stems are at an angle when you repot.

S. elegantissima (formerly classed as *Dizygotheca*), false aralia or threadleaf, is a lacy-leafed and faintly bronze-toned species that makes a refined and elegant impression. Its single stem sometimes attains 5 to 6 feet with foliage spreading from 18 to 24 inches, though this slow-growing plant may stay under 2 feet for years. Its leaves divide, fanlike, at the end of long stems into long, very narrow leaflets (4 to 9 inches long and barely ½ inch wide) with notched edges. As the plants mature, those leaflets become 12 inches long and 3 inches wide. Plant several false aralias in one pot for a mass effect; otherwise, their naturally unbranched form looks sparse.

TOP: *Schefflera elegantissima*
BOTTOM: *Schefflera arboricola*

❧ Renew your *Schefflera* one step at a time by cutting only the barest stem to the base each year. This approach stimulates new growth and preserves your plant's overall appearance while improving the shape.

Senecio herreianus

*S*enecio comprises a large and very diverse group of plants, many of which bear absolutely no outward resemblance to one another. It isn't until these plants flower that their relationship becomes clear: they all bear daisylike blossoms. Many houseplants known as *Senecio* have been reclassified more accurately with other genera.

PLANT CARE. Because these plants are so diverse, each species has different cultural requirements.

SPECIES AND VARIETIES. *Senecio* × *hybridus,* the popular gift-plant cineraria, is now known botanically as *Pericallis* × *hybrida.* This living bouquet of perky daisies comes in white, pink, red, purple, and sensational shades of blue; the rounded floral trusses are accented by somewhat coarse, bright green foliage. These plants need bright filtered light, cool temperatures, and constantly moist soil; they are normally discarded after bloom. Numerous hybrid groups exist.

S. rowleyanus and other related species are unusual succulent plants called string of beads. Peculiar green leaves are cupped into beadlike spheres strung along slender stems that can become several feet long; each "bead" is about ½ inch across. Grow these plants in a bright, sunny exposure and water them sparingly. The stems trail gracefully from hanging plants; given ample surface area, they will root at the nodes wherever they touch soil.

SENECIO
(suh-NEE-see-oe)
CINERARIA, GERMAN IVY, KENYA IVY, NATAL IVY, PARLOR IVY, STRING OF BEADS, WAX VINE
Asteraceae

❧ You can grow your own cinerarias from seed sown in late spring. Keep the plants cool, lightly shaded, well watered, and well fertilized for blooms the following winter and early spring.

Senecio × *hybridus*

SINNINGIA

(sih-NIN-jee-uh)

CINDERELLA SLIPPERS, GLOXINIA
Gesneriaceae

∽ *Sinningia* roots begin their growth alongside stems on the tops of the tubers. When you pot dormant tubers, therefore, place them with the stems and traces of roots facing upward, just under the surface of the soil.

Two *Sinningia* hybrids

The best-known houseplant in the *Sinningia* group is the spectacular gloxinia, favored by florists for its showy trumpet flowers. Forerunners and smaller versions of these popular hybrids are the heavy-blooming slipper gloxinias. Smaller still are the miniature sinningias, tiny, long-blooming types; given the right conditions, these can flower nearly constantly. All sizes of these Brazilian beauties have dark green, slightly fuzzy leaves and grow from tubers. Many die down during the winter months and remain dormant until early spring, though some put out new growth before the old stems have withered, never going completely dormant.

PLANT CARE. Gloxinias need bright diffused light and a bit of sunshine (but no harsh afternoon sun), a warm spot about 65° to 75°F (19° to 24°C), high humidity (in dry air, flower buds drop and leaf edges curl and brown), and soil that is constantly moist to the touch (but in soggy soil, roots and tubers will rot). They respond best to tepid water; cold water may shock them and cause pale leaf scars to form.

Give special care to those gloxinias whose stems and foliage die back during dormancy. Fertilize them monthly with a high-phosphorus fertilizer (such as 5-10-10 or 0-10-10) for a limited time only—from the end of the flowering period until the foliage dies back. Thereafter, allow the soil to dry nearly completely. After several weeks of rest in a cool location, dormant tubers will resume growth. As new stems sprout, gradually increase the soil moisture until growth is rapid; when the leaves are full size, keep the soil uniformly moist. Repot every year or two, using a humus-rich, soil-based planting mix in a shallow pot. If conditions are not ideal, cyclamen mites, thrips, aphids, and gray mold may appear.

SPECIES AND VARIETIES. *Sinningia pusilla* is a dainty, everblooming miniature species with leaves and blossoms about ½ inch wide. Some plants have stems, whereas others grow from basal rosettes; both types do best in 1- to 2-inch pots. They like a light dose of liquid fertilizer once or twice a month and thrive in a humid environment, preferring the constant moisture of a terrarium. The long, tubular flowers are lilac with darker accents and a white throat; cultivars come in a multitude of colors.

S. speciosa is a large assemblage of plants that includes the slipper gloxinias, also known as *S. regina.* The slipper flowers tend to face outward, on more compact plants; their tubers may lie dormant for several months after flowering. The more common sinningia is the florists' gloxinia, with upward-facing blossoms. This type has 6-inch or longer oval to oblong leaves and extraordinarily showy flowers that are velvety, bell shaped, and ruffled at the edges. Its blossoms are white and many shades of purple, pink, and red; most have dark dots or blotches with contrasting throats and marginal bands.

The hybrid cultivars of this species are subdivided into named groups according to flower size, shape, and color. Blossoms are either single or double, borne alone or in clusters, and may nod gently or be held upright like trumpets. 'Buell's Blue Slipper' has velvety foliage and numerous curved, trumpet-shaped flowers; 'Double Delight' is a compact, ruffled dwarf that bears large, double blue blossoms with a deep blue throat; and 'Tampa Bay Beauty' is a new cultivar with abundant clusters of trumpetlike scarlet blossoms and dark green foliage.

SOLENOSTEMON

(SOL-uh-NOSS-tuh-muhn)

COLEUS, FLAME NETTLE, PAINTED LEAF PLANT, PAINTED NETTLE
Lamiaceae

Long known as *Coleus,* this popular houseplant and warm-season bedding plant has recently been renamed *Solenostemon scutellarioides.* Its brilliant foliage and easy disposition explain its wide appeal ever since it was collected from Southeast Asia in the late 19th century. Luxuriant, velvety leaves, often ruffled or scalloped, display a rich variety of color in shades of lime, olive, and chartreuse green; dusky rose, magenta, blood red, and deep purple; parchment, peach, yellow, and salmon—a seemingly endless

Solenostemon scutellarioides
Wizard Series 'Scarlet'

litany of combinations that goes on to include unusual oranges, copper, and brown, often in veined and dappled patterns.

Bi- and tricolored heart-shaped leaves are the norm, but some varieties have slender, arrow-shaped or deeply lobed oaklike foliage. The leaves may be 3 to 6 inches long in large-leafed hybrid strains that grow 18 to 24 inches tall, or only 1 to 1½ inches long in dwarf, 12-inch strains.

PLANT CARE. Most important for a healthy coleus is a balance of light intensities—2 to 4 hours of direct sun each day and several more hours of bright light (but bright shade when out-of-doors). Too much sun—as well as heavy shade—can result in faded colors, dropped leaves, legginess, or stunted growth. Coleus is sensitive to cold and prefers temperatures in the 60° to 70°F (16° to 21°C) range, with ample humidity and constant moisture to prevent wilting; it thrives on a humidity tray or with misting when the air is dry.

If you propagate stem cuttings in early fall, you'll have young, vigorous plants each spring. Repot the fast-growing young plants every few months to provide plenty of space for developing roots; fertilize regularly. Mealybugs and spider mites can be a problem.

SPECIES AND VARIETIES. *Solenostemon* hybrids are known by their descriptive cultivar names, such as 'Blusher', 'Copper Glow', 'Dark Frills', and 'Lemon Lime'. Numerous strains exist: Giant Exhibition and Oriental Splendor are both large leafed; Carefree is a dwarf, self-branching type with small, deeply lobed, ruffled leaves; and the Dragon Series has oak-shaped leaves.

✿ Coleus looks fuller if you frequently pinch off its growing tips. Though this removes the flower buds, most indoor gardeners prefer to forgo the blue flower spikes in favor of bushy plants and maximum foliage.

Solenostemon scutellarioides
Striped Rainbow Series

Spathiphyllum moves to the top of the houseplant class when it comes to answering that oft-repeated question, "What's a good plant for foliage and flowers that's also easy to grow?" This 18- to 24-inch plant thrives indoors and blooms reliably with minimal attention. White flowers with a stiff yellow center (similar to those of a calla lily) appear nearly continuously amid the large, dark green, oval to lance-shaped leaves that arch slightly at the ends of slender leafstalks. Lacking a central stem, peace lily leafstalks rise in clusters directly from rhizomes beneath the soil.

PLANT CARE. Low to medium light (never direct sun) and average indoor conditions are perfectly adequate for spathiphyllum. Its tropical foliage looks best, however, if you raise the humidity around it by setting it on a humidity tray. Moisten the soil evenly when the top inch feels dry to the touch; reduce watering when room temperatures fall below 70°F/21°C, and never expose a plant to conditions below 55°F/13°C. Except in winter, feed it regularly with a dilute solution of a balanced fertilizer. As long as new foliage continues to emerge full size, leave the plant undisturbed; but if new leaves stay small, turn the root ball out of the pot to examine it. Repot spathiphyllum only when the roots are too crowded. Plant it in a soil-based, humus-rich potting medium.

SPECIES AND VARIETIES. *Spathiphyllum floribundum* 'Mauna Loa' is a popular cultivar; its white flowers are fragrant and its foliage deep green. 'Mauna Loa Supreme' is taller; its foliage is lighter green and more upright.

S. 'Petite' is a compact form just over 12 inches tall.

SPATHIPHYLLUM
(SPATH-uh-FILL-uhm)
PEACE LILY, WHITE FLAG
Araceae

✿ If you must choose between a bright location and a dim one, place your peace lily in low light. Bright light can burn its foliage and prevent flowering.

Spathiphyllum

STREPTOCARPUS

(strep-toe-KAHR-pus)
CAPE PRIMROSE
Gesneriaceae

❧ Cylindrical, twisted seedpods develop after the streptocarpus flower petals fall. For a longer bloom period, remove faded blossoms before those seedpods form.

A *Streptocarpus* hybrid

Blossoms of the cape primrose resemble those of its close relative, the African violet *(Saintpaulia)*. The most common types available are hybrids, which produce a rosette of strap-shaped leaves up to a foot long. The leaves are somewhat crinkly, resembling primrose foliage but with a fleshy or velvety texture. Flower stalks from 6 to 12 inches tall grow from the center of the foliage rosette.

Two kinds are popular: grandifloras, which produce exceptionally large flowers, and multifloras, which have smaller blooms in larger clusters on more compact plants. Individual blossoms are typically trumpet shaped and flared, usually striped or ruffled, and come in pastel to darker shades of blue, violet, lavender, and red; some have yellow throats. Most types have a fairly long bloom season spanning several months (usually in autumn and winter); others bloom for shorter periods throughout the year.

PLANT CARE. In general, treat a cape primrose as you would an African violet. Shade it from direct sun, but provide bright filtered light. Average indoor conditions are suitable, though increased humidity during the growing season is helpful. Streptocarpus can tolerate cooler temperatures than can African violets, but a drop below 55°F/13°C will induce dormancy. Water freely and apply half-strength doses of a high-potassium liquid fertilizer (such as a 5-10-10 formula) every 2 weeks—except in winter, when plants need less water and no fertilizer. Always allow the soil mix to dry between waterings; too much moisture causes rot. Repot every spring in a well-drained, soilless mix; a shallow container is best for this shallow-rooted plant. Propagate from leaf cuttings. Provide good air circulation to avoid powdery mildew, but never expose a cape primrose to drafts. Mealybugs, aphids, and spider mites sometimes appear.

SPECIES AND VARIETIES. *Streptocarpus* 'Constant Nymph' bears delicate-looking flowers that rise in clusters 6 inches above a rosette of 12-inch-long, deeply veined, strap-shaped leaves. This longtime favorite blooms in pale bluish mauve with darker lines in the throat. 'Electra' is a compact form with bright fuchsia pink blooms; 'Hand Painted' has white blossoms gently ruffled at the rim, a yellow throat, and purple veining that extends into the lower lobes.

SUCCULENTS

Kalanchoe blossfeldiana

Typical succulents are the camels of the plant world: they store water in their fleshy leaves, stems, or roots, maintaining a reserve supply for periods of drought. Members of some plant groups, such as *Agave* and *Yucca*, tend to be more drought resistant than succulent, but are included here for convenience. Cacti are true succulents but constitute a group of their own (see pages 61–66).

PLANT CARE

Because most require no special care and are easy to propagate, succulents are survivors among indoor plants; as such, they've become standards for passing along to friends and family, even for generations. If you are resolute about watering only on demand, which means keeping these plants on the dry side, yours will enchant you for many years.

LIGHT, TEMPERATURE, AND HUMIDITY. Nearly all succulents yearn for as much direct sunlight as possible. If you have a south- or west-facing window, put them there; those in other locations may need supplemental artificial light from a fluorescent tube. During the spring and summer growth periods, give each plant a quarter-turn every week—always in the same direction—to keep it from leaning to one side. Many gardeners like to keep succulents out-of-doors in summer to expose them to bright light and heat—this is particularly important if the indoor environment is air-conditioned. (Aloes, gasterias, and haworthias do best outside in filtered shade rather than in bright, direct sun; indoors, they prefer an east window.) In winter, most like a short rest period in the 50° to 60°F (10° to 16°C) range. Because these plants are native to dry climates, a low-to-average humidity level suits them best.

WATER AND FERTILIZER. Drought-tolerant succulents won't wilt as readily as other houseplants when water is scarce. But don't expect the impossible; taken out of their natural environment and confined to a pot, succulents will die for lack of water just as any other plant will, though perhaps more slowly. A more likely problem—particularly in winter and during periods of slow growth—results from overwatering. These plants need water less frequently than most others do, and they rot easily if the soil mix stays too wet. During growth periods in spring and summer, allow half of the soil to become dry before rewatering. During the natural rest period (usually in winter), don't water at all, or—if you must—only enough to prevent the soil from drying out completely. Many gardeners like to set succulents' pots in shallow water so that moisture is absorbed from the bottom up. This method works well if you are willing to stand watch and ensure that pots never remain in water once the soil surface becomes moist. Always allow excess water to drain away. Watering from below is an especially practical method for plants like echeverias, whose leaves are badly marred if water spatters them.

Mixed sedums

For most succulents, apply a half-strength dose of a water-soluble, balanced fertilizer as you water, once each month during spring and summer only. If flowering is poor, substitute a low-nitrogen product (a 5-10-10 or 0-10-10 formula) for half or more of the feedings.

SOIL AND CONTAINERS. You can use a standard indoor potting soil for your succulents, a cactus mix, or a homemade mix from your own recipe. To ensure fast drainage, add extra coarse sand, perlite, or finely crushed lava rock. You may also want to spread a thin layer of grit or fine gravel over the surface. Because succulents grow slowly, you won't need to freshen the potting mix or repot most of them more often than every few years. It is a good idea, however, to check their roots for vigor and constricted growth each year. If you plant in plastic containers, look to see that the roots have not rotted from excess moisture.

A dish garden of succulent crassulas

Sansevieria trifasciata 'Laurentii'

PESTS AND DISEASES. Pest problems are few, but mealybugs and scale may appear. Check your plants frequently and control problems as soon as you notice them. You may need to discard your plant (a rosette-forming sedum or echeveria, for example) when an insect problem becomes severe. If you refrain from overwatering—which promotes fungal infections—diseases are rare.

Crassula ovata

SPECIES AND VARIETIES

Not all succulents make satisfying houseplants, but of course many do, and these have become reliable standbys in countless households. You'll have more success if you start out with those that love the conditions you already have: perhaps a sedum in a greenhouse window filled with warm sun throughout the day, but a tough sansevieria for a dim interior—or if you have little time to fuss over potted plants. Choose a gray-leafed crassula for contrast against greener foliage, or a stonelike lithops for its surprising shape.

AEONIUM (ee-OE-nee-uhm). One of the most decorative succulents, aeonium looks quite sculptural as it forms its leafy rosettes; on some species, they're held on branch tips, candelabra-fashion. Thickened, spoon-shaped

Aeonium arboreum 'Atropurpureum'

Agave victoriae-reginae

Aloe vera

leaves tend to drop away on the lower stems, leaving the rosettes prominently displayed; the leaves also drop after flowering (which occurs on mature plants only). To rejuvenate leggy specimens you can cut off a rosette, with a short length of stem attached, and root the stem in a planting medium. Give aeoniums bright direct sunlight for best color and shape.

Aeonium arboreum is a 3-foot-tall, treelike plant with 6- to 8-inch-wide rosettes. The leaves of 'Atropurpureum' are beautifully tinted a dark reddish purple.

A. simsii forms broad rosettes in low clumps; its leaves are green with prominent reddish lines. *A. tabuliforme* is also low growing, but wider spreading and platelike; its pale green, pointed leaves form a striking, geometrically patterned rosette as much as 2 feet across; *A. undulatum* is similar, but half as wide.

AGAVE (uh-GAHV-ee). Commonly called century plants, agaves have generous clumps of fleshy triangular or sword-shaped leaves, often with stunning variegation. When well displayed indoors, they become works of art. The leaves of the different species are thin and narrow or wide and fleshy, but always more rigid than soft. Many end in terminal spines and have teeth or hairlike extensions along their margins; others are strictly landscape plants, far too large to grow indoors. Agave clumps die after flowering, which occurs only after many years, but they may leave suckers or offshoots that grow into new plants. Start them out in filtered light and move them slowly into full sun if their foliage doesn't burn.

Agave

Agave parryi, commonly called mescal, forms a compact, cupped rosette about 1 foot wide that looks something like an artichoke. The grayish blue leaves have short, dark brown marginal teeth and a longer, more pointed terminal spine.

A. victoriae-reginae forms a regal-looking blunt rosette (but with terminal spines on the leaves) 8 to 10 inches high and twice as wide. The dark green leaves, 6 inches long and 2 inches wide, are marked with narrow white strips along the margins.

ALOE (AL-oe). A pot of *Aloe vera* on a windowsill has become a household fixture for its use as a burn remedy; others among the hundreds of diverse species and hybrids are more ornamental. All have long, tapering, succulent leaves filled with a mucilaginous sap and lined with spiny or toothed margins; the leaves tend to be softer than they are rigid. Many species bloom prolifically indoors with narrow, reddish orange, tubular flowers on upright stalks.

Aloe aristata, torch plant or lace aloe, is a dwarf plant ideal for indoor culture, at 8 to 12 inches high and wide. Its rosettes are densely packed with 4-inch-long and ¾-inch-wide leaves that are spotted with prickly dots and end in whiplike threads. In winter, orange red flowers appear in clusters on 1-foot spikes.

A. vera (or *A. barbadensis*) is the medicinal aloe that forms clusters of stiff, upright rosettes. The spear-shaped, gray green leaves are sometimes spotted; their margins have shallow, pinkish red teeth. Given little water in winter and ample amounts in summer, the leaves will stay plump; they may burn in direct sun.

CRASSULA (KRASS-yuh-luh). These South African succulents have become indoor classics, loved for their unusual shapes and for the thickened leaves that make them so drought tolerant. Most crassulas can remain in the same pot for several years, requiring little more than the basics—a bright location all year and ample water and fertilizer during the growing season.

Crassula arborescens, silver jade plant, is a shrubby plant similar to the popular shiny green jade tree *(C. ovata),* but smaller and slower growing. The red-rimmed and

Crassula 'Morgan's Beauty'

rounded, bluish green leaves fill well-proportioned branches on this stout-stemmed species. Where space is available, this crassula is a standout indoors: it grows about 4 feet high and wide. Its white or pink star-shaped flowers rarely appear.

    C. ovata (also known as *C. argentea* and *C. portulacea*) is the familiar jade tree. This excellent houseplant loves to spend summers out-of-doors but must be brought in before the first frost. Clusters of pink, star-shaped flowers bloom profusely from November through April, blanketing the foliage in a hazy veil. You can easily trim the thick, woody stems and branches to control the size of your jade tree, or you can root stem sections to start over with a smaller plant when your shrubs become too large. This species has glossy, medium green leaves, though several cultivars offer variations. 'Dwarf Green' has darker leaves tipped in burgundy; 'Tricolor' adds pinkish tints.

ECHEVERIA (EK-uh-VEER-ee-uh). The echeverias, many of which are known as hen and chicks, are mostly small, rosette-forming plants that adapt easily to container culture. The rosettes may be short and flattened or mounded in colonies—or they may unfold at the ends of long stems. Some species, such as chenille plant *(Echeveria pulvinata)*, branch and trail; others, like *E. peacockii,* form solitary rosettes. Their fleshy leaves are green or gray, often marked with deeper colors. Bell-shaped, nodding flowers in pink, red, or yellow are borne on tallish stalks. Give them bright light (direct sun if possible), water them sparingly, and keep the foliage dry to avoid unsightly watermark scars. You can propagate them easily from leaf cuttings, stemmed rosettes, or offset plantlets.

    Echeveria elegans, called Mexican gem and Mexican snowball, is a stemless echeveria that forms nearly white rosettes (actually, a bluish gray coated in dusty white) about 4 inches across. Offsets are borne on stems that protrude from under the bottom leaves. The flowers are pink and yellow.

    E. secunda, one of the hen-and-chicks plants, forms gray or bluish gray rosettes up to 4 inches across that produce offsets freely. The leaves of *E. s. glauca* are tinted purple and are faintly edged in purplish red.

TOP: *Echeveria peacockii*
BOTTOM: *Echeveria pulvinata*

EUPHORBIA (yew-FOR-bee-uh). Known as spurges, the euphorbias comprise one of the largest of all plant groups. They make a bold statement and are prized as decorative elements for their striking forms, textures, and colors. Many look like cacti, but their spines emerge directly from the stem rather than from the specialized depression (or areole) characteristic of the cactus family. Slow-growing plants, they stay in scale with their surroundings and are reasonably tolerant of dry indoor air. Be cautious when handling euphorbias; besides prickly surfaces, most have an acrid, milky white sap that can irritate the skin and cause pain if it makes contact with open cuts or gets into eyes.

Euphorbia canariensis

Euphorbia esculenta

    Euphorbia greenwayi is an exciting euphorbia with vertical rainbow striations fading from green to blue to whitish gray. The four-sided stems have toothed and spined margins outlined in reddish brown. *E. trigona* 'Rubra' is similar, but taller and often only three sided. *E. canariensis* has several four- to six-sided vertical branches.

    E. obesa, gingham golf ball or living baseball, is a dwarf and spineless orb that is well described by its common names. Reddish brown or purplish plaid bands appear as it grows; small flowers are borne at the apex.

GASTERIA (gas-TER-ee-uh). These compact, succulent-leafed plants form flattened clumps or rosettes. They are familiarly called ox tongue or bow-tie plant for their thickened leaves, which are often swollen at the base and dotted with warty, white bumps. They may be mottled, blunt tipped or pointed, flat or twisted. These

Gasteria

plants thrive in the warm, dry air of most homes, making them ideal houseplants. Gasterias need less light than do most other succulents, never require fertilizers, and should never be exposed to direct sun. Tubular flowers appear on stalks in late spring.

HAWORTHIA (hah-WUR-thee-uh). Spiraling rosettes of triangular leaves taper to a point on most haworthias. The foliage on some species is short and broad at the base; on others, longer and more dagger shaped. Generally the leaves are covered with translucent patches, lines, or raised white tubercles. Their fascinating shapes and bumpy textures as well as their need for medium to low light make haworthias popular indoors. Their blooms are less attractive than their foliage, so you may want to remove flower buds as they appear.

Haworthia attenuata

Haworthia attenuata, wart plant, is an extremely variable species—stemless or short-stemmed, it has bright white, warty bands on the undersides of dark green, spear-shaped leaves. *H. fasciata,* the zebra haworthia, is similar but has shorter leaves.

H. venosa tessellata is a popular mat-forming species with short, recurved, triangular leaves that are checkered on their upper surface and warty beneath. Greenish white flowers appear in spring.

KALANCHOE (KAL-uhn-KOE-ee). Grown principally as houseplants, members of this Mediterranean plant group owe their popularity to broad-leafed succulent foliage and long-lasting blooms. Dozens of diverse species and varieties are available—some quite unusual, such as the fuzzy panda plant or pussy toes, *Kalanchoe tomentosa.*

K. blossfeldiana is a bushy plant with broad, ovate, glossy green foliage. It normally produces clusters of bell-shaped flowers in winter—but, like many other florists' favorites, its hybrids can be manipulated into bloom at any time. For the home gardener, it's easiest to summer a kalanchoe out-of-doors and bring it in before the first frost; it should then provide ample blossoms for the winter holidays.

K. pumila is a sprawling, gray-leafed plant frosted in chalky white. The lax stems, to 12 inches long, are effective in a hanging basket. Pinkish flowers lined with purple appear in clusters in late winter. *K. fedtschenkoi* is also suitable for hanging.

ABOVE: *Kalanchoe tomentosa*
LEFT: *Kalanchoe fedtschenkoi* 'Marginata'

LITHOPS (LITH-ops). Looking very much like their common names—stone face or living stones—lithops are barely recognizable as live plants. They grow naturally among the pebbles and rocks of southern African deserts. The thick, stubby leaves on either side of a central fissure have a flattened, translucent panel on top, usually marked with dots or blotches; a daisy-like flower appears out of the fissure each summer. Grow these remarkable plants in very small pots or in a dish garden in direct sun year-round. They require no fertilizer, scant water in summer, and must have no water at all during their winter rest.

Lithops olivacea

SANSEVIERIA (SAN-suh-VEER-ee-uh). Called mother-in-law's tongue, snake plant, and bowstring hemp, among other colorful names, sansevierias are among the most treasured of all houseplants for their tough resilience in the face of adversity. They can withstand most indoor conditions except overwatering. (If their leaves scorch, remove them from direct sun.) Usually stemless, these plants produce spreading clumps of narrow or broadly ovate leaves from underground rhizomes; their foliage is either upright or arranged in flattened rosettes. As the plants expand, you can easily divide them or take leaf cuttings to increase their numbers. Flowers rarely appear indoors—but if they do, they'll delight you with their white wispy clusters and evening perfume.

Sansevieria trifasciata is the familiar tall species, with marbled horizontal stripes in pale green and leaves to 4 feet high (though usually less) and 2 or more inches wide. Its leaves stand rigidly upright or spread slightly at the top. 'Laurentii' adds yellow marginal stripes to the picture. Low-growing cultivars have leaves similar in texture but confined to low, spreading rosettes 5 to 10 inches wide. 'Hahnii', bird's nest sansevieria, has medium green leaves with crosswise silvery mottling; the foliage of 'Golden Hahnii' is dark green in the center with broad, golden yellow bands along the leaf margins.

Sansevieria trifasciata 'Hahnii'

SEDUM (SEE-duhm). Known as stonecrops, sedums from many parts of the world are prized by collectors for their success in potted culture. These succulents thrive nearly as well in humid climates as they do in their more arid native habitats. Foliage color and shape—as well as plant size and habit—vary widely within this group; you may want to assemble samples of various types in your succulent garden. Give these plants full sun and no fertilizer; replace aging plants with young ones propagated from stem cuttings.

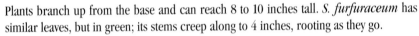

Sedum morganianum, the burro's tail, has numerous stems that are best displayed by hanging. Overlapping waxy, pale gray green leaves spiral around long stems that can reach 3 to 4 feet. This species needs richer soil than do most sedums, liberal water, and two or three doses of fertilizer during the summer. 'Burrito' is a compact version. *S. sieboldii* also trails; its stems are shorter and its leaves thinner and flattened.

Sedum sieboldii

S. rubrotinctum is called pork and beans for its reddish brown tint and bean-shaped leaves. Plants branch up from the base and can reach 8 to 10 inches tall. *S. furfuraceum* has similar leaves, but in green; its stems creep along to 4 inches, rooting as they go.

Sedum morganianum

SEMPERVIVUM (SEM-puhr-VYE-vuhm). Called both houseleeks and hen and chicks, plants in this group form tightly packed, globular basal rosettes of fleshy, pointed leaves. In summer many-petaled, starlike flowers—pretty, but not showy—bloom on short stalks. Young offsets cluster around the parent rosette to form broad colonies. Many species and hybrid cultivars are available in various sizes and leaf colors—some with frosted tips and margins, others with reddish flushes, dark tones, or whitish hairs.

YUCCA (YUK-uh). Although yuccas have little fleshiness to their rigid leaves and stems, they're classified as succulents under a broad definition (plants that can survive independent of an external water source). Their tough leaves, which protect them against severe drought in natural habitats and landscapes, are valued for contributing dramatic architectural effects indoors. It's best to pass up species with needlelike tips—such as the Spanish bayonets *(Yucca aloifolia* and *Y. baccata)*—in favor of less vicious specimens, unless you can place them safely out of harm's way. *Y. elephantipes*, spineless yucca, is favored for its stiff leaves with toothed margins, and can be grown indoors until it becomes too large.

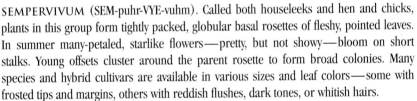

OTHER SUCCULENTS. Among the many unusual succulents is a curious group known as caudiciforms. These plants are named and admired for their swollen stems or bases called caudices (singular: caudex). Many have only a few strangely modified leaves—sometimes fleshy or grasslike—and ravishingly beautiful flowers; some have thorns. All are sensitive to overwatering and must be planted in a fast-draining yet nutritive potting mix. Caudiciforms are found in numerous plant groups including *Brachystelma, Euphorbia, Nolina,* and *Pachypodium.* They add an interesting dimension to a succulent collection. (See "Weird and Wonderful" on page 14.)

Sempervivum globosianum

SHOWY POTS FOR SUCCULENTS

A good use for an unoccupied strawberry jar is to turn it into a tiered display of succulents. Such pots are ideal for displaying the unusual and intriguing forms and colors of these diverse plants. Try composing a study in a single foliage color; or blend blues, greens, aquamarine, rosy reds, and bronzy tones. Choose colorful rosettes with trailing plantlets *(Echeveria, Sempervivum)* to spill out of side pockets; fringed, striped, or bejeweled and pointed rosettes *(Haworthia)* for contrasts; dangling trails *(Sedum)* to cascade down the sides; broad, flat heads *(Aeonium)* and taller, tight clumps *(Aloe, Agave)* for bulk and height. All stand out in sharp contrast to classic terra-cotta pots, and all look right at home indoors in a sunroom or atrium, out-of-doors on a patio or poolside.

SYNGONIUM

(sin-GOE-nee-uhm)
ARROWHEAD PLANT, ARROW-
HEAD VINE, FIVE FINGERS
Araceae

❧ Compact *Syngonium* varieties combine nicely with other foliage plants in dish gardens. Longer, vining types are pleasing when trained on a moss-covered post.

*Syngonium
podophyllum
'Trileaf Wonder'*

Like its *Philodendron* relatives, arrowhead plant, from the tropical Americas, is popular and easy to grow. Young leaves tend to be heart shaped, lengthening as they mature and becoming more arrowhead shaped. Single leaves are produced on slender leafstalks at least as long as the leaves, some up to 12 inches long. Syngonium is notorious for heading off toward the sunlight, growing into a lopsided shape in no time at all.

To keep plants bushy and balanced, pinch their growing tips and give their pot a quarter-turn each week, always in the same direction. Flowers rarely appear on these plants.

PLANT CARE. Give syngoniums bright indirect or filtered light—never direct sun, which can scorch the foliage. Variegated forms need the brightest light. Average room temperatures are ideal; in warmer environments, you should increase the humidity. Throughout

Syngonium podophyllum

the growing season, water your plants when the top inch of soil feels dry to the touch; fertilize them monthly. For a few weeks in winter, water just enough to keep the soil from drying completely; then resume normal care. Repot in a soil-based mix every year or so, when roots fill the containers. Propagate by taking stem cuttings.

Syngonium is long-lived and survives despite poor care. If your plant looks ragged, cut the stems back to an inch or two above the soil. Too much moisture promotes fungal infections. Plants are usually pest free, but watch for sucking insects on leaves and stems.

SPECIES AND VARIETIES. *Syngonium auritum*, also known as *Philodendron auritum* and *P. trifoliatum*, or five fingers, is a thick-textured vining plant with waxy green leaves divided into three to five sections.

S. podophyllum is the most commonly grown syngonium. Its juvenile leaves have three lobes, mature ones five to eleven. Several cultivars exist: 'California Silver Wonder' has narrow, silvery foliage; 'Emerald Gem' has crinkled, dark green leaves veined in pale green on compact plants; 'Trileaf Wonder' has green foliage dusted in silvery gray.

Tolmiea menziesii

Weekend hikers along Pacific Coast trails are often amazed to encounter piggyback plants growing there—but finding these popular plants in an indoor garden is no surprise. You can purchase tolmieas in many stages of maturity, but try to buy a young specimen with rich green foliage. Tolmiea adapts most easily to interior environments when it is small—and growth is so rapid (to 1 foot high and wide) that you'll have a large plant in no time.

Piggyback plant is grown for the interesting way in which it produces plantlets on the tops of mature leaves. Though somewhat rough and fuzzy, the foliage is attractive; the leaves are bright apple green, heart shaped, slightly lobed, and notched along the margins.

PLANT CARE. Tolmiea makes few demands as a houseplant. It grows best in bright filtered light, though indirect light is adequate. In lower light intensities, stems elongate and plants are less compact. Water moderately, enough to keep the soil lightly moist about ½ inch below the surface; water less frequently in winter. Regular but light feeding during the warm seasons encourages good growth and promotes richly colored foliage.

Don't allow your plants to become root-bound; repot them as needed, at least once a year if you have several in one pot. Snip off nicely formed plantlets and root them as replacements for aging plants. Whiteflies and mealybugs are occasional pests, but spider mites are more common. If your plant develops a severe infestation, it's better to replace it than to attempt treatment.

SPECIES AND VARIETIES. *Tolmiea menziesii* is the only species in this plant group. One cultivar, 'Taff's Gold', is also known as 'Maculata' and 'Variegata'. It boasts yellow flecks and cream mottling on lime green leaves.

TOLMIEA
(tol-MEE-uh)
MOTHER-OF-THOUSANDS, PICK-A-BACK PLANT, PIGGYBACK PLANT
Saxifragaceae

❧ To root a plantlet, snip off a mother leaf, leaving an inch or two of stem underneath. Place the stem in the rooting medium so that the union of the baby plant and the leaf is just below the surface.

Tradescantia zebrina

Best known for several species of fast-growing perennial vines from Central and South America, the *Tradescantia* group also includes several plants more familiar under their former names. The purple-striped *Zebrina* and long-leafed *Rhoeo*, for example, have been reclassified and are now included here; like the original *Tradescantia* members, they have flowers with boat-shaped bracts. The leaves are generally small (2 to 4 inches), oblong, and pointed; several kinds have variegated leaves of various hues. Fast growth, easy care, and stunning foliage are the hallmarks of these plants. Nearly indestructible, the vines regrow easily if you cut them back—either severely or just enough to keep growth in check.

PLANT CARE. Most species need bright light (but no direct sun) to produce closely set foliage on long stems. The variegated forms need the brightest light; they can take early morning or lightly filtered sunlight. Warm, humid air is ideal, but most species perform well in typical indoor conditions. Give them extra humidity throughout the year if your air is so dry that their leaf margins brown. Keep the plants away from cold windows in winter. Water them from spring through autumn after the top ½ inch of soil feels dry to the touch; moisten the soil completely, but don't allow it to become soggy. (The plants will rot if the soil is kept too

TRADESCANTIA
(TRAD-ess-KAN-shee-uh)
GIANT INCH PLANT, WANDERING JEW; BOAT LILY, MOSES-IN-THE-CRADLE, THREE-MEN-IN-A-BOAT
Commelinaceae

❧ Trailing plants are traditionally grown in hanging baskets, but you can display tradescantias quite beautifully by training them on a trellis of any shape. For extra flair, combine two species with different foliage colors.

Tradescantia spathacea 'Variegata'

wet.) During winter, water only when half of the entire planting mix is dry. Apply light doses of a complete fertilizer regularly, except in winter.

After a few years, plants generally lose their attractiveness. By propagating them regularly, you'll be able to replace older ones as their lower stems lose leaves. Most stems root quickly and easily in water. Pests and diseases are rarely a problem, but watch for sucking insects.

SPECIES AND VARIETIES. *Tradescantia cerinthoides,* also known as *T. blossfeldiana* and commonly called flowering inch plant, has fleshy, furry stems that spread and lean more than they trail; the leaves are glossy green. The foliage of 'Variegata' is mainly green with bold cream stripes, but some leaves may be solid cream or tinted pink.

T. fluminensis, commonly called giant inch plant or wandering Jew, has long stems that trail or sprawl. Its leaves are 2 to 3 inches long; the small, white flowers are inconspicuous. 'Albovittata' has white stripes on green leaves; 'Aurea' has yellow-striped leaves; 'Tricolor Minima' is variegated in pink, white, and green; and 'Variegata' bears yellow, white, green, or purple stripes.

Tradescantia 'Albovittata'

T. spathacea (better known as *Rhoeo spathacea*) is commonly called boat lily, Moses-in-the-cradle, or three-men-in-a-boat. This species develops sword-shaped, rather erect, dark green leaves with deep reddish purple undersides. Grouping three or more in a pot produces a spectacular effect. Small, white, three-petaled flowers crowd into the purplish boat-shaped bracts, suggesting this plant's common names. The leaves of 'Vittata' (or 'Variegata') are striped in greenish yellow.

T. zebrina, also known as *Zebrina pendula,* is the popular, fast-growing, purple-striped wandering Jew. Its small flowers are purplish pink or violet blue. 'Purpusii' has bronzy purple foliage and pink flowers; 'Quadricolor' bears green leaves banded in white, pink, and carmine red.

TOP: *Persea americana*
BOTTOM: *Mimosa pudica*

PLANTS FOR CHILDREN

Children are fascinated by most unusual phenomena, including extraordinary plants. Try one or more of the species listed here for a simple and fun-filled introduction to plant care. Fast growth and remarkable habits will reward their efforts.

- AVOCADO. Grow a *Persea americana* tree from an avocado seed studded around its middle with three or four toothpicks to suspend it in a glass of water. Pot the seedling when roots form.

- CITRUS. Produce and harvest fruit from a potted orange or lemon tree.

- PINEAPPLE. Start a plant from a pineapple (*Ananas*) top sliced off and set in a shallow layer of soil.

- SENSITIVE PLANT. Touch the foliage of *Mimosa pudica* and watch its feathery leaves fold together.

- SWEET POTATO. Produce mounds of fast-growing, vining foliage in weeks from a sweet potato tuber half-submerged in a glass of water.

- VENUS FLY TRAP. Watch *Dionaea muscipula* or another carnivorous plant attract and ingest insects that cannot escape the lure of its nectar.

INDEX

All photographs, except for those accompanying a main plant entry (the page numbers in **boldface**), are indicated by *italics*.